FORTRESS • 62

SOVIET FIELD FORTIFICATIONS 1941–45

GORDON L ROTTMAN   ILLUSTRATED BY CHRIS TAYLOR

Series editors Marcus Cowper and Nikolai Bogdanovic

First published in 2007 by Osprey Publishing
Midland House, West Way, Botley, Oxford OX2 0PH, UK
443 Park Avenue South, New York, NY 10016, USA
E-mail: info@ospreypublishing.com

ISBN 978 1 84603 116 8

Editorial by Ilios Publishing, Oxford, UK (www.iliospublishing.com)
Design by Ken Vail Graphic Design, Cambridge, UK
Typeset in Monotype Gill Sans and ITC Stone Serif
Index by Alison Worthington
Originated by United Graphics, Singapore
Printed and bound in China through Bookbuilders

09 10 11 12 13   12 11 10 9 8 7 6 5 4 3

A CIP catalogue record for this book is available from the British Library.

FOR A CATALOGUE OF ALL BOOKS PUBLISHED BY OSPREY MILITARY AND AVIATION
PLEASE CONTACT:

NORTH AMERICA
Osprey Direct, C/o Random House Distribution Centre, 400 Hahn Road,
Westminster, MD 21157
Email: uscustomerservice@ospreypublishing.com

ALL OTHER REGIONS
Osprey Direct , The Book Service Ltd, Distribution Centre, Colchester Road,
Frating Green, Colchester, Essex, CO7 7DW
E-mail: customerservice@ospreypublishing.com

www.ospreypublishing.com

Acknowledgements and image credits

The author is indebted to Nick Cornish of Stavka Military Image
Research for his aid in obtaining and selecting photographs from
Russian archives. The following abbreviations refer to the image
credits in this book:

CMAF	Central Museum of the Armed Forces, Moscow
RGAKFD	Fonds of the RGAKFD, Krasnogorsk

Distances, ranges, and dimensions are given in the metric system.
To covert these figures to the US system the following conversion
formulae are provided:

centimetres (cm) to inches	multiply centimetres by 0.3937
metres (m) to feet	multiply metres by 3.2808
kilometres (km) to miles	multiply kilometres by 0.6214

Artist's note

Readers may care to note that the original painting from which
the colour plate on page 56–57 in this book was prepared is
available for private sale. All reproduction copyright whatsoever is
retained by the Publishers. All enquiries should be addressed to:

Brian Delf, 7 Burcot Park, Burcot, Abingdon, Oxon OX14 3DH, UK

The Publishers regret that they can enter into no correspondence
upon this matter.

The Fortress Study Group (FSG)

The object of the FSG is to advance the education of the public
in the study of all aspects of fortifications and their armaments,
especially works constructed to mount or resist artillery. The FSG
holds an annual conference in September over a long weekend
with visits and evening lectures, an annual tour abroad lasting
about eight days, and an annual Members' Day.

The FSG journal FORT is published annually, and its newsletter
Casemate is published three times a year. Membership is
international. For further details, please contact:

The Secretary, c/o 6 Lanark Place, London W9 1BS, UK
Website: www.fsgfort.com

Contents

Introduction   4

Soviet defensive doctrine   6

Building and manning the defences   12

Establishing the defence   14

Defensive firepower   21

Building the fortifications   25
Construction materials • Construction principles

A tour of the fighting positions   31
Riflemen's positions • Machine-gun positions • Mortar and anti-tank gun positions
Trenches • Troop bunkers and shelters • Camouflage techniques

The test of battle   50
Developing a company strongpoint • The defence of cities • The defence of buildings
Forest and swamp defences • Winter defences

An assessment of Soviet field fortifications   62

Further reading and research   63

Glossary and abbreviations   63

Index   64

Introduction

The Red Army of Workers and Peasants[1] considered itself an offensive army that followed a doctrine of highly mobile warfare, and which was capable of attacking deep into the enemy's rear. While such doctrine was made possible by Russia's vast open lands, it was often hampered by limited military resources and the mindset of the Soviet officer corps, whose members were resistant to change and often failed to see the wider picture. The Red Army's theory of defensive field fortifications and obstacles was largely based on lessons learned in World War I, all of which affected their design, construction, camouflage, integration into the terrain, and dispositions on the field. Despite the Red Army's reluctance to engage in defensive operations, they were forced to undertake large-scale ones in the face of the overwhelming German blitzkrieg between 1941 and 1945, even though they had benefit of endless depths of country to withdraw into.

This book provides a study of the field fortifications constructed by combat troops defending the frontline during the Great Patriotic War. The larger, permanent fortifications, such as the Stalin and Molotov lines, are beyond the scope of this book and will be dealt with in a forthcoming Osprey Fortress title. This book focuses on temporary, crew-served weapons positions and individual and small-unit fighting positions, built using both local and occasionally engineer-supplied *matériel*. The frontline soldiers (*frontoviki*) mostly built these positions and obstacles themselves, sometimes under the guidance of engineers. However, extensive use was made of penal battalions and forced civilian labourers to prepare defences behind the front for units to fall back to, and thousands of men, women, and children turned out to dig trenches, anti-tank obstacles, and other fortifications.

Impressed civilian labourers dig an anti-tank ditch. Hundreds of thousands were employed in such tasks and were instrumental to the defence of the Motherland. They turned out for work regardless of age, sex, or physical condition. The clothing and footwear of the women here are clearly inadequate for this type of work. (CMAF)

[1] See Osprey Men-at-Arms 216: *The Red Army of the Great Patriotic War 1941–45.*

The Union of Soviet Socialist Republics was, in its time, the largest country in the world, spanning 11 time zones. The terrain of the western part was as varied as the ethnic groups that populated the country. In the far north it was rocky with low hills, ridges, ravines, valleys, and lakes, and the countryside could be barren, sparsely vegetated, or forested. Most of the central region was densely forested and in many areas there were swamps and marshes. The approximate southern boundary of the forested areas was on a line running north-eastwards covering Lvov–Kiev–Kursk, although there were some large forested areas below this. The vast Pripet Marshes lay on the southern edge of this region; they partly dried out in summer, but the autumn and spring rains made them all put impassable. In the south and stretching far eastwards were the sprawling, seemingly endless steppes. In the extreme south lay the Caucasus Mountains. The USSR's rivers ran in all directions and were more often bordered on both sides by marshes, swamps, and bluffs, which provided greater obstacles than any river itself. Prior to World War II, its road and rail systems were primitive and spaced far apart, and its towns and villages were widely scattered. Its dirt roads were churned up by German heavy traffic and were turned into quagmires with the coming of the rains. Even the rail system worked against the German invaders, since the Soviets used a wider gauge.

The climatic extremes were just as varied as the terrain. Long, hot, dusty summers were followed by a short, rainy autumn, and a long, brutal winter with heavy snowfall and temperatures plummeting as low as -52°C (-61.6°F). A short spring ensued with more mud caused by snowmelt and rain. The terrain and climate were brutal in equal measure to the attacker and the defender alike, and required both to be highly adaptable in terms of tactics, obstacles, and camouflage methods.

Permanent fortifications were established by the Red Army on the borders with Poland, the Baltic States, and Romania between 1926 and 1939, including around Leningrad and Kiev.[2] There were also permanent fortifications in the Far East facing Japanese-occupied Manchuria, and when the USSR occupied eastern Poland in 1939 they began construction of defences along the new border (the Molotov Line). There were also coastal defences on the Baltic and Black Sea coasts and around the few other key ports. These reinforced concrete and stone fortifications were heavily augmented by field fortifications. Nineteen 'fortified region' (Ukreplennye Raiony) units were established to man these permanent fortifications – brigade-sized units comprising a varied number of machine-gun artillery battalions, armed and equipped with anti-tank rifles, 45mm anti-tank guns, 50mm and 82mm mortars, 76mm field guns, and searchlights. For the most part, though, they were manned by only a small number of battalions, often only a quarter of what was needed. The fortified regions could be 50–150km wide and up to 16km deep, including the forward outposts and obstacles. Many of the defences were obsolete by the time of the German invasion; their machinery and equipment were worn out, many of their weapons had been moved elsewhere or placed in storage, their obstacles had deteriorated, and they were overgrown with vegetation.

Frontoviki rush to their fighting positions through a trench. Most armies of the period had largely abandoned the trench as the primary fighting position, but the Red Army retained it. The fighting positions in this instance are log covered and offset from the main trench, a common characteristic of Soviet trenches, as are the low, wide parapets. (CMAF)

---

[2] The Germans called this the 'Leningrad Line', but the defences were actually part of the Stalin Line border defences. This will be dealt with in more detail in the forthcoming Fortress title *The Stalin and Molotov Lines: Soviet Western Defences 1926–41*.

Soviet defensive doctrine

Soviet defensive doctrine was an amalgamation of the French-influenced tactics of the Czarist period, and the lessons learned during the ill-fated battles around Port Arthur in the 1904–05 Russo-Japanese War, trench warfare with the Germans 1914–17, the Russian Revolution with its city fighting and mobile guerrilla warfare 1917–22, and the border fighting with Poland in the 1920s. In the 1930s the Red Army began a programme of modernization with a focus on mechanization and the ability to attack deep into enemy lines. Marshal Mikhail Tukhachevsky's reforms, which called for deep operations by combined-arms forces, began to be implemented in the early 1930s. Although he fell from Stalin's favour, his theories had far-reaching effects on the Red Army's offensive and defensive doctrine. The disastrous 1939–40 Winter War with Finland in itself had little impact on defensive doctrine, but Marshal Semyon Timoshenko's reorganization of the army into smaller, more manageable units did in fact affect defensive doctrine. Timoshenko also studied the doctrine and organization of western armies and this too had its influence. He added more tanks and reinstituted the traditional harsh discipline. This as much as anything stiffened the army's ability to defend successfully.

Soviet defensive doctrine had to take several factors into consideration. It assumed that any enemy attacking the USSR, especially from the west, would do so with superior forces; that the enemy would have to attack on a broad front with the main attacks conducted at multiple points; and that the enemy's lines of communication would be extended and vulnerable. The Red Army would be supported by internal lines of communication, but it was realized that they too would be hampered by the excessive distances and limited rail and road networks. The defence, which might not have to be established on all fronts, was considered as only a temporary measure until the offensive could be commenced to drive the enemy from Soviet territory. Other factors affected Soviet defensive thought. Terrain could be ceded by frontline forces (which were heavily mechanized and possessed a great deal of artillery) and they could withdraw into the immense interior. This also gave the USSR time to field additional forces and produce war *matériel*, while also extending the enemy's supply lines. And then the enemy would have to contend with the effects of the Russian winter on their troops, horses, and equipment – something the Germans did not consider

A *frontoviki* rapidly digs a hasty rifleman's fighting position. Digging from the prone position under fire was obviously a much slower process than digging while kneeling. (Author's collection)

The author dug this rifleman's hasty firing position with an entrenching tool in 10 minutes to the dimensions prescribed in the Soviet manual. The thickness of the loose earth parapet would be ineffective against rifle fire. For scale, the brick measures 9 x 19cm. (Author's collection)

adequately. The Germans assumed that both sides would cease major operations until the following spring, ignoring the lessons learnt by the Swedes, French, and the Germans themselves just 24 years earlier, or even what had recently happened to the Soviets in Finland.

Red Army defensive doctrine stressed the following:

- The defence was to be first and foremost an anti-tank one with all available anti-tank rifles, anti-tank guns, artillery, mines, and hand-delivered anti-tank weapons, and incorporating natural and manmade obstacles.
- Divisions and regiments would establish mobile reserves of anti-tank guns and engineers to be employed in the direction of the enemy's main attack.
- Infantry, anti-tank guns, and all artillery within range would make every effort to defeat enemy armour in front of the main line of resistance (MLR).
- Each artillery battery would establish an observation post to detect and warn of the approach of enemy armour. The artillery would be prepared to engage enemy armour at direct-fire ranges from 800m.
- Anti-tank guns and machine guns would provide the basic fire system in the defence.

Zones of engineer obstacles would be established as far as 12km forward of the MLR at the order of division or corps/army[3] commanders. Obstacles were to be emplaced in such a pattern that they would not always be laid out parallel with the MLR, but would mislead the enemy as to the MLR's actual location and orientation, so that the enemy would approach it obliquely, thus allowing flank shots by anti-tank guns.

An essential part of the defence was the establishment of combat outposts, called the 'security service', forward of the MLR. Besides providing early warning of the enemy's approach and the ability to hamper his patrols, they served to confuse him as to the actual location of the MLR. The outposts would be sufficiently strong, armed with anti-tank guns, and supported by dedicated artillery batteries from behind the MLR, which all served to confuse the enemy into thinking that he was entering the MLR. The enemy would thus deploy into slow-moving battle formations early, and expend artillery into unoccupied areas. Outposts also had engineer detachments to emplace mines in the path of advancing tanks, or on roads after the reconnaissance element had passed and before the main attack force arrived. The outposts were detached from the rifle

---

[3] At the beginning of the war Soviet armies possessed two to four corps, each with two to four divisions. In 1942 corps were generally disbanded and armies now directly controlled divisions, of which six to eight were assigned to each army.

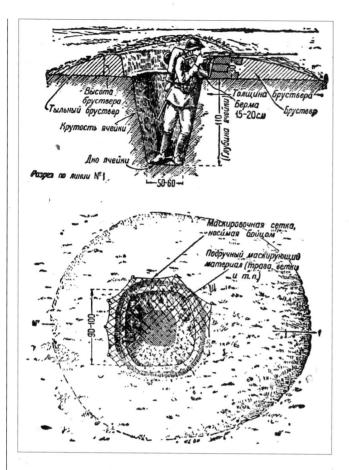

The rifleman's standing fighting position yielded sufficient spoil to build an all-round parapet. The kneeling position was similar in design. Note the individual camouflage net and how the rifleman pushes it upward with his helmet to fire. It would be garnished with local vegetation. (Author's collection)

battalions manning the actual MLR. When withdrawn, the outposts would fall back past the frontline defenders and form counter-attack 'shock groups' or occupy secondary positions. The shock groups would attack tanks with anti-tank rifles, shaped-charge anti-tank hand grenades (which only had a 15–20m throwing range), incendiary bottles[4] and demolition charges; they would use smoke candles to blind tank crews; and they would lay mines in their paths. They also made extensive use of the large numbers of captured German hand-emplaced 3kg magnetic hollow charges and (after 1943) captured Panzerfausts. A small number of changed-charge anti-tank rifle grenades were employed, but these were relatively ineffective and were withdrawn in 1942.

A division's defensive troops were positioned in depth throughout its assigned sector, with multiple lines of defence, designated 'fire sacks' (sometimes called a 'fire trap' or 'anti-tank area'), shock groups, and reserves. Fire sacks were essentially ambush sites on routes that armour might follow if they broke through and continued into the rear area. They were established on terrain that restricted tank manoeuvre, for example forest roads, marshy ground, stream crossings, causeways, within villages, ravines, defiles, and so on. They were covered by multiple anti-tank guns and were backed up by the presence of shock groups. Effective camouflage of the firing positions was essential, and guns were positioned to achieve flank shots where possible. The order to open fire was given by the overall commander, as surprise was essential.

Multiple fire sacks were planned ahead of enemy contact, but they were not always manned. Anti-tank and artillery[5] units (both towed and self-propelled) were deliberately assigned more than one fire sack, and would move to the designated one once a breakthrough occurred. These were not small operations: a two-battalion regiment would commonly be employed. Ideally two batteries would be positioned on both sides of the route and another at the far end to close off the enemy's passage. The sixth battery was held in reserve, to be committed if the enemy changed direction or managed to break out. Engineers would emplace obstacles and mines to close off the fire sack, and indirect artillery fire would be concentrated on it. It was realized that often the enemy would not be destroyed in a fire sack; however, it slowed him down and debilitated him while the anti-tank reserve (*Protivotankovyy Rezerv*) was positioned.

Anti-tank strongpoints were established within regimental and divisional sectors on terrain that was difficult for armour to negotiate. The strongpoints would be further protected by mines, manmade obstacles, and artillery. The Soviets relied more on the effects artillery had on tanks than most armies. Indirect artillery was usually considered none too effective against tanks, as the chance of a direct hit was remote. Most armies employed artillery mainly to separate enemy infantry from the tanks, thus allowing anti-tank guns and their

---

[4] What the Soviets called 'bottles with flammable mixture' were not referred to as Molotov cocktails, as it was not 'politically correct' to make light of their leaders' names.
[5] In 1942 light artillery regiments and battalions, and anti-tank batteries of infantry and cavalry regiments were re-designated 'anti-tank artillery' to emphasize their dual role.

own infantry to engage the tanks unhindered – tanks without accompanying infantry being extremely vulnerable to close-in attack. The Soviets counted on large amounts of artillery, which included multiple rocket launchers, to separate the infantry; to destroy or damage at least some tanks; to create craters, destroy buildings, and fell trees – thus impeding the advance; to restrict the enemy's visibility with smoke and dust; and to cause confusion. A later requirement of Soviet artillery design was for it to be capable of engaging armour; to accomplish this, artillery weapons were provided with sufficient traverse, direct lay sights, and anti-tank ammunition. Anti-tank guns were required to fire high-explosive (HE) rounds for use against personnel and light fortifications; in fact, the 37mm anti-tank guns were replaced with 45mm versions in order to provide a more effective HE round.

The importance was stressed of camouflaging positions and obstacles, including rear-area facilities. Positioning these on rear slopes or deep within forests was a common practice. Dummy strongpoints and artillery positions would be constructed in the division sector, with the aim of attracting the attention of the enemy's artillery and air attacks.

The Soviet division would launch counter-attacks with its infantry and anti-tank reserves, reposition artillery for direct fire, and use sappers to create obstacles and lay minefields in the path of an enemy breakthrough, if the strongpoints and shock groups were unable to halt it. If enemy armour managed to penetrate deep into Soviet positions then army-level reserves and aircraft would be committed.

Soviet doctrine specified two kinds of defence. The (preferred) 'centralized defence' was deployed to hold key approaches to critical positions employing mutually supporting strongpoints. Secondary approaches were covered by direct and indirect fire by massed artillery. A large mobile reserve was held to contain or counter-attack any breakthroughs, under direction of the overall commander; however, this was seldom available. Logistics facilities were positioned centrally to support the strongpoints and the reserve. The 'decentralized defence' was only employed when insufficient forces were available, in extremely rugged terrain where defending units were separated, or on secondary fronts where major attacks were unlikely. The defensive positions or strongpoints were usually smaller and more numerous than in the centralized defence. They had to be self-supporting, and each contained its own infantry, anti-tank guns, artillery, engineers, logistical support, and a small reserve. Local commanders had the latitude and authority to execute counter-attacks. The overall commander held only a small reserve. Rather than employing one-third of the division's infantry units in reserve (that is, one of its three regiments as was normal in the German and Western Allied armies), the Soviets usually maintained only one-ninth – a single rifle battalion.

The porous decentralized defence had little hope of holding out against large-scale attacks. It was often considered necessary,

The hasty anti-tank rifle position was simply a widened rifleman's position. The bipod was buried in the parapet. This weapon is a single-shot 14.5mm PTRD-41. (Author's collection)

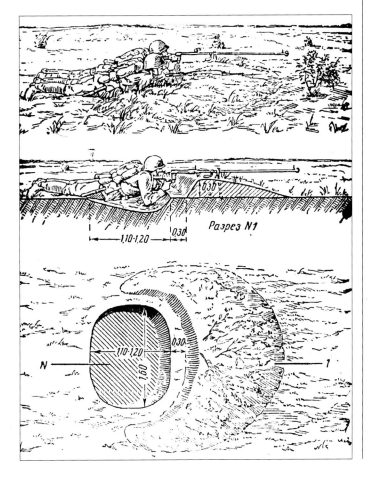

An anti-tank ditch

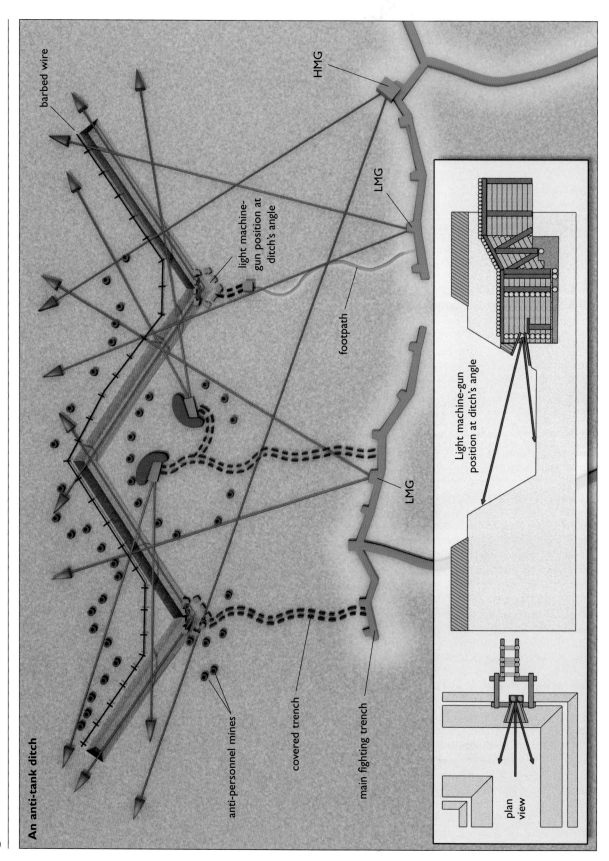

barbed wire

light machine-
gun position at
ditch's angle

HMG

LMG

footpath

LMG

anti-personnel mines

covered trench

main fighting trench

Light machine-gun
position at ditch's angle

plan
view

An anti-tank ditch

Anti-tank ditches provided an effective, although labour-intensive, means of halting or delaying enemy tanks. However, they also provided cover to attacking enemy infantry. Several methods were used to deny the enemy this cover. The ditches were dug close to the forward fighting positions, allowing heavy and accurate fire to be laid. Mortar fire was registered on the ditches. Barbed wire was placed in front of the ditches and sometimes behind them.

Anti-personnel mines were sometimes placed inside or before ditches along with booby traps. Light machine-gun or rifle/submachine-gun positions were built into the ditches' sides at angles. To protect the blind-to-the-surface positions inside the ditch, rifle positions were placed forward of the main trench line. The ditches were also covered by interlocking machine-gun fire. Covered trenches sometimes linked the ditch positions and their forward covering positions to the main trenches.

Anti-tank rifle crews are shown here taking up hasty positions. They are armed with the semi-automatic 14.5mm PTRS-41. The shear bulk and size of these weapons can be appreciated in this photograph. The assistant gunners are armed with 7.62mm PPSh-41 submachine guns, but could be armed with rifles. (Author's collection)

though, because there were simply not enough troops available to defend the many passes, gorges, ridges, and hills in a mountainous area, or to man continuous lines in dense forests and swamps. At other times it was permitted due to the paucity of German forces facing them in a particular area. Another reason the centralized defence was preferred, especially early in the war, was the lack of experience among small-unit commanders. They simply just did not have the skills to manage all the attached support units necessary for a decentralized defence.

It must be noted that while defensive positions were first and foremost established as anti-tank defences,[6] defensive lines on terrain restrictive to armour (forests, swamps, hills, and mountains) employed the same basic principles. In such instances, fewer anti-tank weapons would be employed and anti-tank obstacles emplaced only where necessary. Some anti-tank guns were still employed, but mainly as anti-personnel weapons.

Even with relatively mobile reserves, mobile anti-tank artillery, large mechanized units at the front, and an offensive doctrine calling for highly mobile operations, the Red Army's defensive doctrine relied on brute force and was comparatively static. The concepts of mobile or elastic defence, as practised by the Germans, did not exist. A mobile defence provided flexibility and the ability to move aside and conduct counter-attacks on the enemy's exposed flanks. The lack of experience amongst Soviet commanders did not allow for this. Additionally, rifle divisions lacked sufficient transport to move infantry units, support units, and their supplies to conduct a mobile defence, and nor were there sufficient tank and mechanized units backing the armies.

[6] See Osprey Elite 124: *World War II Infantry Anti-Tank Tactics*.

Building and manning the defences

When the Germans launched Operation *Barbarossa* on June 22, 1941 the Red Army was totally unprepared. Even though the Germans had underestimated the strength of the defenders, the blitzkrieg steamrollered into Soviet territory with unprecedented speed. Soviet tank formations were devastated, aircraft were destroyed on the ground, and the leadership thrown into confusion and panic. Soviet commanders, owing to a recent devastating purge, were not up to the challenges facing them and overall troop training had been deficient. Soviet soldiers dropped their rifles and ran, surrendering and deserting by the hundreds of thousands. Tanks, artillery, trucks, and supplies were abandoned. Drastic means were resorted to in the effort to halt the flight to the rear and restore the front. Commanders were shot by commissars for withdrawing without authorization, well-armed 'barrage battalions' were positioned behind 'unstable' divisions with orders to shoot retreating troops, and penal units were formed of 'soldiers and sergeants who have broken discipline due to cowardice or instability'. These units were deployed at the most difficult sectors of the front, thus giving the soldiers an opportunity to 'redeem their crimes against the Motherland by blood'.

It was through such severe measures, as well as a combination of patriotism and hatred for the invader, that the front was gradually stabilized. The Soviet soldier developed a reputation for conducting a tenacious and stubborn defence. He could disappear into the ground at a surprising speed, and minefields and barbed-wire entanglements suddenly appeared where none had been the day before. Captured German positions would be transformed overnight with the weight of the defence shifted to the east side, and huge numbers of mines would be laid rapidly on the avenues of approach. In one instance it was reported that the Soviets laid 20,000 mines in one day in front of a captured German position.

A PTRD-41 anti-tank rifle crew covers a road into their unit's position. The parapet is constructed entirely of sods of earth. An irregularly shaped embrasure was less obvious at longer ranges than a neat square or rectangular one. The section leader is equipped with 6x B-6 binoculars. (RGAKFD)

Dummy positions and obstacles were built to mislead the enemy as to the strength and density of the defence, as well as to attract artillery and air attack. Such positions could be set among real frontline positions to make the sector look more densely defended, to the rear of forward positions to make the defence appear deeper, or even forward of actual positions for the same reason, causing the enemy to deploy early and thus slowing their attack. To ensure realism a few troops and small numbers of crew-served weapons were emplaced within dummy strongpoints. Sometimes elements of reserve units partly occupied decoy positions. The strength of manned strongpoints would be varied to mislead the enemy, with troops and crew-served weapons shifted between them and the day and night 'shifts' changed.

Positions were well camouflaged. Peasants and other locals excelled at making them appear natural and blending them into the surrounding terrain, whereas conscripted city soldiers were less able in this area. Obstacles and positions were often emplaced on reverse slopes to conceal them from ground observation, and to silhouette the attacker against the sky as he crested the high ground.

The Soviet soldier was renowned for withholding fire until the Germans were within effective range. The original doctrine called for weapons to engage the advancing enemy at their maximum range. However, it was found to be more effective to 'ambush' him with a surprise burst of fire from all weapons within optimum range and from multiple directions. Reserve (alternative) firing positions were prepared for all crew-served weapons, not only for occupation when the primary position became untenable, but to mislead the enemy as to the location and numbers of weapons by constantly shifting positions. Supplementary positions were prepared to allow weapons to cover other sectors, such as the flanks and rear. Weapons could also be repositioned to cover the gaps between strongpoints.

Prior to 1941, Red Army units had undertaken little training in the construction of field fortifications and obstacles, and there were few soldiers, even among officers, with experience in engineering and construction. They had to learn construction skills in the midst of the unrelenting German invasion. Engineering committees were established and studies made at the front, and new manuals were issued in 1942 and 1943 on fortifications, obstacles, and camouflage. These were largely updates of 1930s manuals, but incorporated recent lessons learned. Regardless of fortification and obstacle designs specified in manuals, actual practices in the field often differed owing to terrain and weather conditions, available materials and tools, the tactical situation, personal preferences, and battlefield experience or the lack of it. In short, there was a great deal of improvisation.

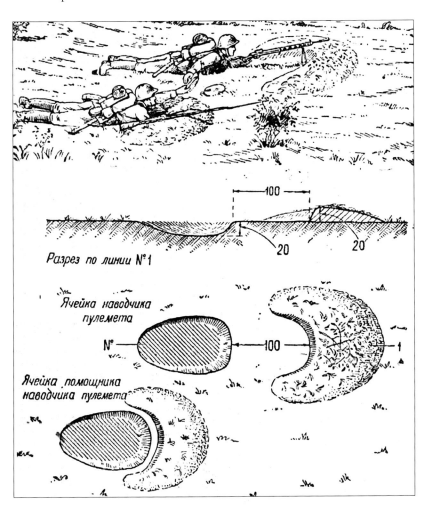

Разрез по линии №1

Ячейка наводчика пулемета

Ячейка помощника наводчика пулемета

The hasty two-man light machine-gun position was usually emplaced in the centre of the rifle section's position, although some sections possessed two 7.62mm DP machine guns. (Author's collection)

Establishing the defence

The division was the main echelon around which the defence was based. It contained all the necessary assets: infantry, artillery, anti-tank, engineers, signals, and logistics. It could be augmented by other units, especially anti-tank and artillery, from army level. At the beginning of the war, the average width of a rifle division's defensive sector was 8–12km, with a depth of 4–6km. In sectors assessed as the most likely for the enemy main attack, divisions would be assigned narrower frontages and would establish more in-depth defences. Conversely, divisions in less threatened sectors would defend fronts three times wider than was normal (see Table 1 below). They would also receive additional support beyond what those in less likely attack sectors would be given. Due to this 'prediction of attack', it has been said that 80 per cent of the available Soviet forces defended 10 per cent of the front.

The Soviets defended the ground they took. They did not give up seized areas to 'dress up' the lines, nor did they withdraw and deny such areas to the enemy using fire only. A unit was assigned an area to defend based on terrain, enemy forces, unit capabilities, reinforcing units, and availability of reserves and supporting fire. Because of these factors infantry unit frontages varied greatly. Table 1 indicates the prescribed defensive frontages and depths; they were slightly wider in the pre-war regulations.

Table 1: Prescribed Soviet defensive frontages and depths

Echelon	Frontage	Depth
Section (squad)	40–50m	35–45m
Platoon	300m	250m
Company	700m	700m
Battalion	1–2km	1.5–2km
Regiment	3–4km	2–4km
Division	6–10km	4–6km

The division would ideally establish an 'outpost line' as far as 9–17km from the MLR, but it could be closer due to the proximity of German positions. There were instances, though, when the outpost line could be established further out, for example when a new defensive line had been established in preparation for a major withdrawal from more forward positions.

Next came the 'security line', 1–2km forward of the MLR. It provided early warning of enemy approach and anti-reconnaissance screening. The personnel manning this line were from the reserve companies of the division's forward battalions. They would be deployed in small strongpoints and outposts, sometimes heavily armed with anti-tank weapons and supported by artillery and mortar fire. It was common for strongly manned outposts and strongpoints to be forward of dummy positions while weaker outposts were in front of the main positions.

The MLR was tasked with halting the enemy's attack. Units were not to withdraw unless ordered, which was seldom the case. It was preferred that units be destroyed, as this would inflict greater losses of manpower, equipment, and time on the enemy. Counter-attacks and blocking positions would deal with any enemy breakthroughs. Typically two rifle regiments were employed forward, with one to the rear in the form of a second line of defence as opposed to a reserve. The divisional mobile reserve, though, was often drawn from this second-line regiment. Besides the mobile reserve (if established), there was also an anti-tank reserve.

The regimental sectors contained a varied number of mutually supporting strongpoints capable of all-around defence. The strongpoints could be manned by full battalions, two companies, or a single company. They were emplaced in depth and there might be smaller company and platoon strongpoints and outposts protecting the approaches to the main strongpoints. The organization of strongpoints and defensive positions was prescribed as follows:

- Positions should be established in depth.
- Each defensive position and its internal parts should be capable of all-round defence.
- The defence should be supported by planned counter-attacks.
- The fire plan should be designed to provide fire sacks in sectors subject to attack.

The Soviets were firm believers in the strongpoint. It was found early in the war that anti-tank guns scattered along a thin defensive line to cover a wide frontage did not work. A thin defensive line could be penetrated at any point, with the enemy rushing through the gap into the rear areas to destroy command posts, communications centres, artillery, reserves, and logistics facilities. Providing depth to the defence was essential, and self-contained strongpoints with concentrations of anti-tank guns and emplaced in depth through the defence zone, including multiple strongpoints on the main roads of advance, were much more effective. In 1941 anti-tank defences typically had a depth of only 2–3km. By the time of Kursk in July 1943 the depth had increased to 8–12km.

Strongpoints were heavily protected by manmade defences blended into natural obstacles such as dense forests, swamps, marshes, streams, deep mud, large rocks, gullies, steep slopes, railway embankments and cuts, and so on. Anti-tank mines would be laid on routes of armour approach with anti-personnel mines dotted among them to hamper clearing efforts. The areas between strongpoints were connected by anti-tank and anti-personnel obstacles and mines, and were covered by outposts, patrols, and fire. All obstacles were covered by pre-planned artillery and mortar concentrations, as well as by rifle, machine-gun, and anti-tank fire. Obstacles, especially those protecting the rear of strongpoints, were to have gaps in them to allow Soviet counter-attack forces through. These gaps were covered by machine-gun and mortar fire, and could be closed by quickly laid mines (i.e. laid above ground, preferably among brush and high grass). The rear

A 7.62mm DP light machine-gun crew mans a hasty two-man position, having recently won an occupancy dispute. Normally the assistant gunner was to the gunner's right. An anti-tank rifle crew mans a more advanced position. It was common for frontline positions to be scattered so irregularly. (RGAKFD)

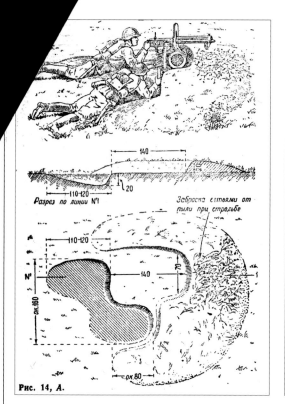

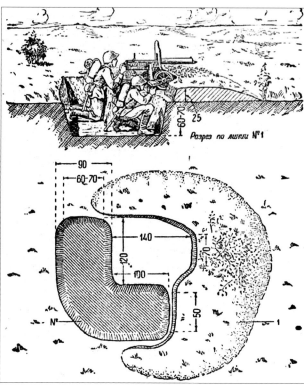

Рис. 14, А.

areas of strongpoints often had only a few scattered fighting positions, rather than being fully defended. If the strongpoint was overrun this prevented the enemy from rapidly preparing a dug-in defence to meet the inevitable counter-attack. Once the enemy overran a strongpoint, artillery and mortar barrages would immediately be ordered, and lifted only when the counter-attack was driven home. The idea was to inflict casualties on the exposed enemy, prevent him from reorganizing and redistributing ammunition, and hamper his digging in.

Strongpoints varied greatly; their form depended on the terrain (including that of the approaches), the assessed size of the enemy force, the available time and construction materials, the weather conditions, and the available supporting weapons.

By 1943 a typical battalion strongpoint found in the battle of Kursk[7] included four to eight 45mm anti-tank guns, nine to twelve 14.5mm anti-tank rifles, two to four 82mm mortars, and possibly two to four dug-in, self-propelled guns or tanks. The battalion would be augmented by a sapper platoon with demolition explosives and mines. Within the battalion strongpoint would be company strongpoints with three or four 45mm anti-tank guns, two or three anti-tank rifles, a sapper section, a submachine gun section, plus tank-destroying shock groups with Molotov cocktails and demolition charges.

Countless kilometres of anti-tank ditches were dug, often by impressed civilians. These could be many kilometres in length and in multiple lines (as per the three- and four-tier anti-tank ditch network west of Stalingrad – today known as Volgograd). Ditches 3–4m deep and 4–6m wide were common. When multiple lines of ditches were dug, lateral connecting ditches were dug to compartmentalize the network. Removed earth was usually piled in front of anti-tank ditches, in effect making them deeper and steeper. Ditches were often dug on forward slopes of ridges and gently rising ground to gain advantage of upward inclines. Along fordable rivers and streams the Soviet-side shore embankment

[7] For a full account of this battle, see Osprey Campaign 16: *Kursk 1943*.

was cut back to create a vertical barrier. While fighting trenches followed terrain contours and avoided geometric patterns, anti-tank ditches were distinctly angular. Rifle, machine-gun, or anti-tank positions were often dug into the angled turns of anti-tank ditches to provide enfilading fire down their length. Since German infantry would use anti-tank ditches for cover and as attack jump-off lines, it was found to be better to locate ditches closer to the MLR in order to provide more effective aimed fire when they emerged to attack. The ditches were also mined and booby-trapped, strung with barbed wire inside and on the forward edge (and sometimes to their rear), and had mortars registered on them. Streams were sometimes dammed in low areas to create flooded areas 100m or more across and 1–3m deep. Even if shallow, the saturated ground bogged down tanks and slowed enemy infantry.

Regardless of the unique aspects of any given front, its terrain, and the circumstances of the defenders (which would all affect the form of any defensive works), at the unit level (defined by the Soviets as regimental level and below) common principles for the establishment and conduct of the defence were employed down to section (or squad) level.

High ground was of course desirable for defensive positions as it provided longer fields of observation and fire, and made it harder for the enemy to fight his way uphill. Even an elevation of a couple of metres was an advantage. Caution had to be exercised though: placing defensive positions on the geographic crest was undesirable as it silhouetted positions against the sky and made them easy to target via map reconnaissance. Positions were placed on the forward slope of a hill or ridge on the 'military crest' (one- to two-thirds of the way up the slope). Care had to be used when selecting the exact line and how high up the slope they were placed. If located too high some positions might still be silhouetted against the sky by an observer at the base of the hill. Whether the forward slope was concave (curving inward) or convex (curving outward) was important. On a (seldom regularly) convex slope, if the positions were too high a blind spot or 'dead ground' was created that could not be observed or fired into. The same considerations applied to the location of reverse-slope defences. A convex reverse slope might deny observation of the geographic crest from positions lower down the reverse slope. This would handicap the defender since one of the benefits of a reverse slope defence was the ability to fire on attackers as they were silhouetted passing over the crest.

The enemy had to be destroyed before his attack developed too far, or at least forced to withdraw or dig in. This was accomplished by concentrating all available weapons on the enemy along his routes of possible attack, before he reached the MLR. If the enemy managed to gain a foothold in a strongpoint or on favourable terrain from which he could launch further attacks, it was essential that he be driven out or destroyed as soon as possible. Heavy fire would be placed on these positions and counter-attacks launched immediately, even if the force was insufficient to carry the enemy foothold. The idea was to keep the enemy off balance, and hamper his reorganization and consolidation. There was also the chance that the attackers might be in worse shape than thought and could be defeated.

The Germans would typically launch their main attacks along main roads, but did not necessarily keep to the roads while advancing; once engaged, they would deploy to the flanks. Having overrun a Soviet position and broken through, at least part of the force would continue on the road, if a lack of resistance

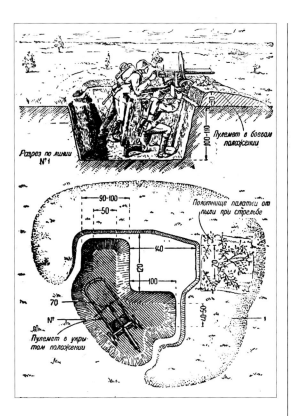

The water jacket on the heavy machine gun was easily punctured by fragments. Additional space was dug into the rear to place the gun inside the position. To reduce dust raised by muzzle blast, a common practice was for the crew to urinate on the parapet. (Author's collection)

This light machine-gun position has a firing platform revetted with vertical posts. The embrasure has two ports, due to the need to support the sod-and-plank head protection. This is a DT, the tank machine-gun version of the DP modified for infantry use. Note a board is provided to support the bipod. (RGAKFD)

permitted, in order to increase the speed of penetration. For this reason the Soviets emplaced anti-tank strongpoints, and even individual anti-tank guns and dug-in self-propelled guns, adjacent to such avenues in depth.

Effective employment of the different weapons organic to an infantry regiment required a great deal of experience – something often lacking among Soviet infantry commanders early in the war. Those who survived the Germans, their political officers, and NKVD barrage battalions became proficient at recognizing the different capabilities and limitations of each type of supporting weapon, such as light and heavy machine guns, anti-tank rifles, anti-tank guns, mortars, regimental guns, supporting artillery, and anti-aircraft guns employed in the ground role.

Light anti-tank guns (37mm and 45mm) were positioned well forward, but not beyond the infantry frontline, with progressively larger-calibre guns (45mm, 76mm, and 85mm) in subsequent lines. Large-calibre guns could be positioned forward to cover key avenues when deemed necessary. Anti-tank guns were covered by infantry and anti-tank rifles. Anti-tank rifles were positioned in pairs or larger groups within 50m of each other. Sometimes anti-tank guns were positioned 100–150m apart along the front, but more often they were positioned in groups; for example, four guns could be positioned in a diamond pattern to provide all-round fire. The interval between the guns varied depending on the terrain and vegetation density. Camouflage and alternative positions ('reserve positions') were greatly emphasized, and fire was held until tanks were at least within 600m to avoid prematurely revealing positions. Anti-tank guns and artillery were expected to fire until overrun. The destruction of large numbers of tanks was considered a successful defence even if the guns were lost. The Soviets were strong proponents of mathematical calculations to forecast military actions and unit capabilities. It was calculated that a 76mm field gun, often employed in the anti-tank role, required an average of six rounds to knock out a tank, and that it would destroy two or three tanks before it was itself destroyed. A 45mm gun required 12 rounds to destroy a tank and would knock out one or two before it was lost. The 6 to 12 rounds needed to knock out a tank were not all necessarily fired at the same tank, as this figure included rounds that were fired at other tanks, or missed, or were deflected.

Anti-tank rifles were highly thought of by the Red Army, even though most armed forces considered them obsolete by 1940/41, and few remained in use in any theatre from 1943. Besides lacking penetration (due to improvements in armour), anti-tank rifles were heavy, awkward, and punished the gunner with a hard recoil. The single-shot PTRD-41 and semi-automatic PTRS-41 weighed around 40lb., and were over 6ft long. The Soviets enjoyed a greater degree of success with anti-tank rifles, as these were of larger calibre than most (14.5mm = .57-cal.), used a tungsten carbide-cored incendiary bullet, and were employed in large numbers. Indeed, the Soviets retained them throughout the war, and with some success. Most countries allocated anti-tank rifles on the basis of one per rifle platoon. The Soviets issued them in larger numbers: 27 in the regimental anti-tank company, a company of 16 in the battalion (later reduced to a platoon of nine), and a battalion of 36 in the division. Headquarters, artillery, and other support units were also issued anti-tank rifles for self-defence. Their tactics emphasized manoeuvring them to obtain flank and rear shots, and employing them in groups to engage tanks from different directions; for example, it was recommended that 10 anti-tank rifles be employed to engage a German platoon of four or five tanks.

While Soviet doctrine emphasized the role of armour as a deep-striking manoeuvre force, some self-propelled guns and tanks were dug in. This was especially true of the SU-76 Suchka ('Little Bitch') 76mm self-propelled gun. Only a small number of the early model SU-76s were built. They had a fully enclosed gun compartment, but were notoriously unreliable. Huge numbers of SU-76Ms were built from 1943. They had an open-topped gun compartment, often with an open rear, light armour, and no defensive machine guns. The open compartments made them vulnerable to grenades, small arms, and air bursts. However, the open compartment did reduce casualties from Panzerfaust hits, as it relieved blast over-pressure. Other self-propelled guns (the SU-85, SU-100, SU/ISU-122, and SU/ISU-152) were employed in a similar manner. Owing to the SU-76's vulnerability it was not uncommon for it and other self-propelled guns to be dug in to cover roads. Multiple positions were prepared along roads for surviving guns to fall back to. This way their mobility was put to good use in situations where towed anti-tank guns would be easily overrun. The doctrinal mission of self-propelled artillery in the defence was to constitute the mobile fire reserve, which would support the infantry and tank counter-attack. They could also be part of the anti-tank reserve.

There were actually two kinds of dug-in positions for self-propelled guns and tanks. A firing position in which the AFV was in hull defilade allowed the turret to be rotated, if applicable, and the main gun fired; it required the AFV to reverse out, as the front and sides were protected by a parapet and the pit's depth. The other position was a deeper, sloped pit into which the AFV was reversed to provide a turret defilade that protected it from artillery and helped conceal it from air observation. It had to be camouflaged to achieve this purpose.

The Red Army artillery was tasked with destroying or neutralizing enemy forces that were encircled, or were attacking defensive positions. It was employed on a massive scale, in numbers and weight far exceeding that used by the World War I western Allies. Soviet artillery had lost many pieces in the war's early days, but in some ways this proved beneficial as they were replaced by more modern examples. Due to a lack of experienced artillery officers and surveying equipment, and poor communication and target acquisition methods, artillery units were placed under centralized control in large formations. The rifle division's modest artillery regiment was heavily reinforced with

This heavy machine-gun position is elaborately constructed with a plank gun platform, and tongue-and-groove notched logs. A lattice-work of vines covers the embrasure, to support camouflage and deflect grenades and demolition charges. (CMAF)

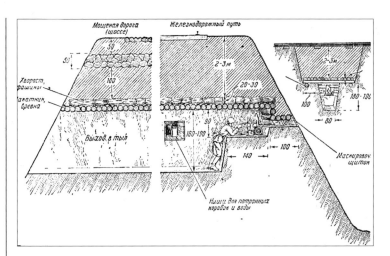

Мощеная дорога (шоссе), Железнодорожный путь, 50, 50, 100, 2-3м, 2-3м, 20-30, 100, 180-190, Хворост, фашины, 80, накатник, бревна, 90, 160-190, 100, Выход в тыл, 140, Маскировоч щитон, Ниши для патронных коробок и воды

This is an example of a cut-and-fill machine-gun position dug into a railway (right) or road (left) embankment. In the example to the left, two layers of rocks have been added as shell-burster protection. (Author's collection)

army-level units, including artillery divisions. Such a division could have 12 regiments of light, medium, and heavy artillery and heavy mortars. There were also significant numbers of independent regiments and battalions. Besides conventional towed artillery, to which the Soviets allotted a great many tractors and trucks as prime movers, there were anti-tank artillery and multiple-rocket launcher units. There were situations in which 200–300 artillery pieces and mortars were available per kilometre of front.

Camouflage efforts and all-round local security was continuous during the development of defensive positions. The camouflaging of rear-area facilities, especially artillery positions, command posts, communications centres, and supply dumps, was given special attention because of the initial air threat. Despite the Soviets gaining gradual control of the air, nonetheless they continued to take precautions as the Germans were not driven completely from the sky. Great pains were taken to camouflage supply routes near the front from the eyes of German artillery observers. The routes were screened to conceal vehicle and troop movements, and dummy supply dumps and facilities were widely constructed in the rear areas.

The Soviets employed a wide variety of anti-personnel and anti-tank obstacles. In an effort to conceal them, the obstacles would be emplaced along natural contour lines, on low ground, on reverse slopes, along the edges of fields, and among brush and high grass. Anti-tank ditches, especially the long, multiple-line systems, which were commonly dug into forward slopes, were impossible to conceal, but the knowledge of their presence often forced the Germans to attack on other routes, which, if properly planned, would be more heavily defended. Terrain was important in that swamps, marshes, forests, rivers, streams, gullies, ravines, broken and rocky ground slowed or halted armour. While the Soviets realized the importance of placing obstacles, including minefields, under observation and fire, there were frequent incidents where this was deliberately not done. Anti-tank and anti-personnel mines and booby traps were often emplaced on the approaches to and among obstacles. The Soviets used metallic mines as other armies, but they also made extensive use of wooden ones, which were impossible for the Germans to detect with mine detectors. The Soviets also had a fixed flamethrower (FOG) that could be electronically fired from a distance to cover obstacles.

While large numbers of Soviet troops surrendered, others sometimes held out in well-prepared strongpoints. The Soviet soldier's physical and mental toughness contributed to his ability to resist. To the Germans they were seemingly immune to suffering, hunger, thirst, and the climate. The Germans used tanks, assault guns, anti-tank guns, and artillery wheeled up to point-blank range and firing over open sights to blast apart heavily constructed bunkers. Pioneer troops employed flamethrowers and demolition changes, including container (satchel) charges, pole charges (charges fixed to the end of a pole allowing them to be placed high against walls or shoved through embrasures), extended charges (charges placed end-to-end on long planks and pushed under barbed wire), and shaped-charges to make holes in concrete fortifications. They used smoke grenades and candles to blind the fortifications as they closed in. The Germans did not like this close-in fighting, but it was the only way to root the Russians out of their holes. It was even worse in the forests and swamps, to say nothing of what it was like in the rubble of cities.

Defensive firepower

The Soviet rifle division, the main formation on which the defence was based, changed much during the course of the war in regard to strength, structure, and allocations of weapons. The USSR began the war with a traditionally structured division as found in many European armies, that is, large and cumbersome. Several tables of organization were in use at any one time, as existing divisions often retained their organization while newly raised divisions were organized under new tables. For this reason only a cursory examination of basic divisional structure can be provided here.

The rifle division consisted of a headquarters; three rifle regiments; an artillery regiment; machine-gun, anti-tank, engineer, signal and medical battalions; reconnaissance, chemical defence and motor transport (supply unit) companies; and an anti-aircraft battery.

The early divisions were cumbersome in that they had too many organic supporting weapons units. Many of these were reassigned to higher echelons in order to streamline the divisions and to provide for a more agile and manageable formation for inexperienced commanders. The divisions were fairly well balanced in the mix of supporting weapons, though generally they were deficient in mortars and in some cases machine guns. Anti-tank guns were too light, but this was a common deficiency in all armies of the period; the abundance of anti-tank rifles was an attempt to compensate for this. Artillery was of comparatively light calibre, and both truck and horse-drawn wagon transport was very limited. At full strength a division had up to 200 trucks and specialized vehicles and 1,700 horses. Most artillery was horse-drawn. While trucks were

Impressed civilians complete a heavy machine-gun bunker. Camouflaging sod is being laid on the bunker's roof. While the bunker is large, note the small size of the rock-faced embrasure. Civilians were directed by engineer officers. (RGAKFD)

Table 2: Soviet rifle regiment, December 1942

Unit	Weapons	Unit	Weapons
Regimental HQ		Submachine Gun Company	
HQ Platoon		Regimental Gun Battery	4 x 76mm guns
Anti-aircraft Platoon	3 x 12.7mm MGs	Mortar Battery	7 x 120mm mortars
Horse Reconnaissance Platoon		Anti-tank Gun Battery	6 x 45mm AT guns
Foot Reconnaissance Platoon		Anti-tank Rifle Battery	27 x AT rifles
Sapper Platoon		Signal Company	
Chemical Defence Platoon		Transport Company	
Rifle Battalion (x 3)		Medical Company	
Battalion HQ		Veterinary Hospital	
Signal Platoon		Weapons Repair Workshop	
Rifle Company (x 3)	12 x LMGs, 1 x HMG, 2 x 50mm mortars	Regimental Trains	
Machine Gun Company	9 x HMGs		
Mortar Company	9 x 82mm mortars		
Anti-tank Gun Platoon	2 x 45mm AT guns		
Anti-tank Rifle Platoon	3 x AT rifles		
Medical Platoon			
Battalion Trains			

provided to tow anti-tank guns and other heavy weapons, there were only enough to tow the guns and none available for ammunition reserves, unit equipment, headquarters personnel, and supplies within an anti-tank unit. Organic logistics support was minimal with the division relying heavily on army-level support.

As with the division the rifle regiment varied in structure, personnel and weapons allocation over time. In most armies the infantry regiment consisted of three battalions, usually with three rifle and a weapons company with heavy machine guns and mortars, a regimental anti-tank company and perhaps an infantry gun or light artillery company, and possibly a service company. The Soviet rifle regiment was in effect a miniature division replicating support and service units found at division level. Rather than three supporting regimental companies, the Soviet regiment had up to eight such companies and additional smaller support units. While giving the regiment significant additional capabilities, it was difficult for inexperienced commanders to control and its logistical requirements were increased. The December 1942 rifle regiment is provided in Table 2 as an example.

The rifle battalions also possessed significant support units and heavy weapons. The Soviet battalion had nine medium mortars (whereas most battalions of the period possessed four or six). Even though there were anti-tank

Types of obstacles

Anti-tank ditches
Anti-tank walls (concrete and stone)
Rail and timber barricades
Log and stake barricades
Interlocking felled trees (abatis)
Steel hedgehogs (three railway rails or I-beams)
Log hedgehogs (three logs wrapped with barbed wire)
Elongated rocks planted vertically in rows
Concrete blocks set in rows
Single- and double-apron barbed wire fences
Tanglefoot barbed wire obstacles
Spanish rider (barbed wire-wrapped portable wood
  frame barrier, a.k.a. kniferest, chevaux de fries)
Sharpened stakes driven in at an angle
Flooded areas (dammed streams)

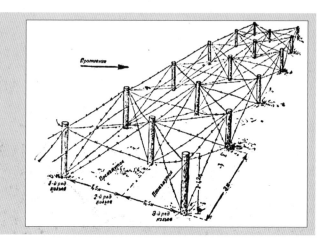

rifles and guns at regimental level, the battalions possessed a small number for their own use in case the regimental weapons were being used to support other battalions. The regiment's mortars, eighteen 50mm, twenty-seven 82mm, seven 120mm, plus four 76mm regimental guns provided a great deal of indirect fire support, a valuable asset in the defence. Its 36 anti-tank rifles and twelve 45mm anti-tank guns were also adequate, and the regiment would probably have additional anti-tank rifles and guns attached from division. Typically a platoon each of heavy machine guns and 82mm mortars, each platoon having three weapons, were attached in support of a rifle company, but they could just as likely be allocated to companies on an uneven basis depending on the expected enemy avenues of approach. This abundance of supporting weapons at company, battalion, and regimental levels was ideal for the strongpoint defence as it meant ample weapons were available to arm numerous strongpoints.

Rifle companies were organized into a small headquarters, a medical section, three rifle platoons, a mortar platoon with three 50mm mortar sections, and a single heavy machine-gun section with a water-cooled 7.62mm SPM-10 Maxim or air-cooled SG-43 machine gun (often not provided).

The rifle platoon had a four-man headquarters and four nine-man rifle sections (squads). Earlier 11-man sections were fielded. There were two heavy sections with two light machine guns and two light sections with one gun. With losses, platoons might field three or even two sections with the remaining machine guns more or less evenly allocated between them. Owing to shortages there might be only one machine gun per section. The standard rifle was the bolt-action 7.62mm Mosin-Nagant M-1891/30. The semi-automatic 7.62mm Tokarev SVT-40 had been officially adopted as the standard shoulder weapon, but they were few in number. A small number of early units were armed with it; a few were sometimes issued to rifle platoons alongside bolt-actions. The section leader was usually armed with a 7.62mm pistol-calibre PPSh-41 or PPS-43 submachine gun, nicknamed the 'balalaika'. The standard light machine guns were the 7.62mm Degtyarev DP and DPM (from 1944), fed by a 47-round pan magazine from which got its nickname of 'the record-player' (*proigrivatel'*).

Two divisional units important to the defence were the machine-gun and anti-tank battalions. The machine-gun battalion had three companies each with nine SPM-10 Maxims plus an anti-tank rifle company with 12 rifles for close-in defence of the machine guns. The anti-tank battalion had three

This heavily constructed machine-gun bunker is built of logs, covered with earth, and topped with a layer of rocks. The exposed rock covering and large-plank embrasure make it conspicuous. (RGAKFD)

An example of a prefabricated, reinforced concrete, one-man fighting position. There was no standard design, and could be of varying shape and sizes. Some only had a frontal portion. Similar 'mini-bunkers' were also made for machine guns. (US Army)

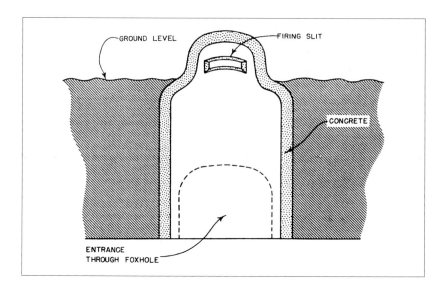

batteries of four 45mm anti-tank guns. These began to be replaced by 57mm guns in late 1943. The heavy machine guns reinforced strongpoints and the anti-tank guns were emplaced in depth through the divisional sector.

Although changes were made during the war, a division artillery regiment normally had three artillery battalions with 76mm guns and 122mm howitzers. This was considerably lighter than its German counterpart, which had three battalions of twelve 10.5cm howitzers and a fourth with twelve 15cm howitzers and four 10cm guns. In 1941 divisional artillery regiments had only two battalions, each with eight 76mm guns and four 122mm howitzers. In early 1942 a third battalion was added, but with only one each of 76mm and 122mm batteries. The anti-aircraft battery had six 37mm guns. Divisions, though, would often be heavily reinforced with non-divisional artillery and mortar regiments including Katyusha multiple-rocket launcher units.

The Red Army also organized rifle brigades beginning in 1941 in an effort to speed up the fielding of units. Brigades could be raised and deployed faster than complete divisions. These brigades comprised three rifle, two mortar (light/medium, heavy), artillery (76mm), anti-tank, and signal battalions plus reconnaissance, submachine gun, sapper, transport, and medical companies. While possessing a great deal of firepower, they were weak in riflemen. Some 250 brigades were raised by the end of 1942, after which no more were organized. Most were rolled into divisions in 1943. In a strongpoint defence the brigade could only hold a narrow frontage, not much more than a regiment, but with all the available firepower the strongpoints would be extremely well armed and an in-depth defence easily established.

Soviet artillery ranges
This listing provides the ranges of the most common artillery pieces. Large-calibre mortars were considered artillery. While newer models of a given calibre were fielded, older models remained in use, some to the war's end. The 76mm field guns and 122mm howitzer were the standard divisional artillery. (All '76mm' weapons were actually 76.2mm.)

Artillery/mortar	Range	Artillery/mortar	Range
76mm F-22 field gun (1936)	4,200m	122mm A-19 gun (1937)	20,500m
76mm F-22 USV field gun (1939)	4,200m	152mm M-10 howitzer (1938)	12,400m
76mm ViS-3 field gun (1942)	13,300m	152mm D-1 howitzer (1943)	12,400m
76mm M-27/39 regimental gun (1939)	3,000m	152mm ML-20 gun-howitzer (1937)	17,200m
76mm M-43 regimental gun (1943)	4,200m	152mm BR-2 gun (1935)	27,000m
107mm M-60 gun (1940)	17,500m	160mm MT-13 mortar (1943)	5,100m
120mm HM-38 mortar (1938)	6,000m	203mm B-4 howitzer (1931)	16,000m
122mm M-30 howitzer (1938)	11,800m		

Building the fortifications

Construction materials

The Soviets made extensive use of local materials to construct fortifications and obstacles. Cement was available in some areas and it was not uncommon for reinforced concrete bunkers, crew-served weapons emplacements, command posts, and troop shelters to be built on critical avenues of approach – for example, in front of Moscow and Leningrad. Small one- and two-man prefab concrete fighting positions were emplaced in large numbers in some areas. These were frontal sections with an embrasure emplaced in dug-in pits entered by trenches.

The available local materials were dependent on the area of operations, with some offering abundant supplies, and others, such as the steppes of Russia, barren. Many materials had to be transported in with great effort, and peasant cabins and farm buildings were often dismantled for their logs, rafters, doors, and other fixtures for use in fortifications. Much of the timber shipped into this area came from as far away as Siberia, where it was cut by Gulag inmates. This became more difficult to obtain though, as hundreds of thousands of inmates were shipped west and formed into ad hoc rifle units (usually to be quickly slaughtered) or labour units for road and bridge repair, mine clearance, etc. Many were still employed to cut the timber so essential for field fortifications.

Timber was abundant in many areas of Russia. Red Army engineers possessed portable sawmills and also took over local mills to provide rough-cut lumber. Many of the plans for fortifications, shelters, and obstacles provided in the 1942 manual *Infantry Fortifications* (*Fortlfiatsiya Pekhoti*) called for logs, timbers, and dimensioned planks. Fir, pine, and spruce were the most commonly used softwoods. Use was made of birch and larch, both hardwoods. Timber was used for overhead cover, horizontal support beams (stringers), and vertical support posts. The construction plans seldom specified timber diameters, this being left to the builders to determine based on the loads to be borne and what was available. The minimum diameter though was 15–17cm for smaller bunkers, and larger for bigger structures. It is known that logs at least twice this diameter were used in some bunkers and laid in multiple criss-crossed layers up to five thick for protection from heavy artillery.

Crossbeams or roofing logs were not simply laid on the ground. Stringers, in the form of half-buried logs or split logs laid flat-side down beside the pit to be covered by perpendicular logs or planks, were used. The stringers were laid 20–30cm from the lip's edge – further if the soil was unstable. Roof support logs were sometimes staked in place on both sides of the ends.

Dimensioned planks were used sparingly for revetting, (rarely) flooring, doors, shutters, firing port (embrasure) frames, duckboards, ammunition niches, ladders, and steps. Platform-type bunks,

Standard trench designs included the crawl trench (A), the crouching trench (Б), and the full-depth trench (В), in this instance with camouflage netting installed. The enemy is to the right. These designs were common to fighting and communications trenches. (Author's collection)

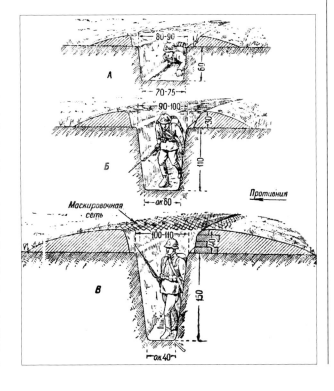

tables, benches, and other furniture were made from lumber and dismantled ammunition boxes. Nails, especially the large spike type required for timber construction, were often scarce. While the exteriors of timber fortifications were banked with earth or were buried below ground level, hits from large-calibre projectiles could create nasty wood splinter injuries.

The Red Army shipped munitions, rations, and other *matériel* in robust wooden boxes, crates, and kegs of all sizes. These were often filled with earth and stacked brick-like to form the interior walls of fortifications, and were also used for revetting parapets. They were braced by logs or timbers or bound by wire to prevent their collapse when the fortification was struck by artillery. Boxes were also disassembled and the boards used to construct embrasures, doors, shelves, and so on. Nails removed from these boxes were highly prized. Steel fuel and oil drums were occasionally filled with earth, although they were supposed to be returned for re-use.

Purpose-made tan burlap sandbags were scarce at the front, but not unheard of. They were mostly used to protect rear command posts, artillery positions, and other rear-area installations. A filled sandbag measured 25 x 25 x 50cm according to a Soviet manual, but they tended to become flattened once stacked to about 20cm thick and 30cm wide. Because of the non-standardized methods of production, dimensions no doubt varied greatly. Burlap ration-shipping and feed bags were frequently used for sandbags. Two layers of sandbags were sufficient to stop small-arms fire and provided protection from mortars. The few sandbags available were mainly used to line firing slots and embrasures in trenches and bunkers. If used to revet the inside of trench parapets that had very loose soil, they were stacked brick-like, only two to three high, with the seams placed next to the wall. Sandbags were also used to provide cushioning for bunker roofs by placing a layer of one to three bags on top of the roof logs and then covering the sandbag layers with earth, including a burster layer if used.

When sandbags were unavailable, as was often the case, earth sod blocks were used. These were removed from the trace of the trench or bunker under construction and set aside. The prescribed dimensions for these blocks were 10 x 20 x 40cm. They were stacked brick-like three high (approximately 30cm) on the forward edge of the trench, leaving a narrow lip, and angled slightly outward. The trench's or position's spoil was then spread out on both sides, 2.5–3m on the

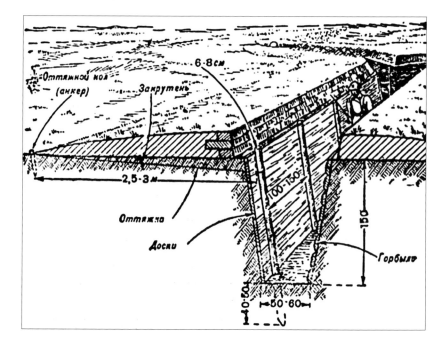

A full-depth fighting trench, revetted with planks held in place by vertical stakes anchored by staked wire. Note the connecting trench in the upper right linking the main trench to a fighting position, the preferred practice. (Author's collection)

front side, about 2m at the rear, and 30cm high. This provided for a low but wide parapet offering protection from small-arms fire.[8] The sod blocks were used only to revet the front parapet as there were not enough available for both sides. The blocks, held together with grass roots, provided more protection than loose soil. The low, wide parapets were supposed to blend into the surrounding ground and coupled with the trench's contour-following trace would make it more difficult to detect. The parapet spoil was supposed to be camouflaged with a layer of ground cover material removed and set aside prior to commencing digging. This included the ground-cover on either side of the trench or position where the spoil would be spread. This natural ground cover included the layer of growing vegetation such as short grasses and weeds or the dead layer of leaves or evergreen needles. In practice, however, the neat prescribed dimensions of the parapets were more varied and irregular, and often left uncamouflaged by replaced ground cover.

Stones were used for construction and revetting, especially in mountainous areas where rock was plentiful. However, the risk of rock splinters from bullet and shell hits was high. Rock walls, if not properly constructed and revetted, could easily collapse when hit by large-calibre shells and shaken by near misses. Fortifications were sometimes made entirely from rock. If available, the outer surface would be covered by soil and camouflaged into the surrounding terrain. Rather than piling or neatly stacking the rock, the preferred method

A posed photograph, no doubt, of a general assisting with the tidying up of a crawl trench. Both square- and round-nose, long-handle shovels were issued. An elbow rest lip was provided behind the parapet for rifle firing. (Author's collection)

was to build log cribs, that is, log cabin-like frames 0.5–2m wide, and filling the space between the log frames with rock. There were many instances where machine-gun or anti-tank gun bunkers were constructed with a reinforced concrete front with embrasures and partially concreted sides. The rest of the sides, interior compartment walls, and the back would be built using rock-filled cribs, and the roof would comprise layered logs, sandbags, and spoil. If a position was roofed with stones, it might consist of a log roof, a thick layer of gravel for cushioning, a layer of stones as the primary protective and burster layer, and then be covered by spoil.

Three types of barbed wire were issued, in spools. The hardened steel, single-strand type had four-pronged, 18mm-long barbs every 75mm and was designed specifically for military use. The twisted, two-strand type had four-prong, 12–15mm-long barbs every 80–100mm. A third type was a thick, spring-steel strand with two-prong, 15mm-long barbs at 20mm intervals; this was used for coiled concertina wire. Captured German and Polish barbed wire was also used. Two types of barbed-wire staples were issued for use on wooden stakes: a U-shaped, 65mm-long staple, and a J-shaped one with 35mm and 70mm shanks. Both had 4mm-diameter shanks. Steel barbed-wire pickets, such as those used by US and German forces, were not issued.

---

[8] A rifle/machine-gun bullet can easily penetrate a metre or more of loose soil or a single layer of sandbags.

Construction principles

Fortified positions were not to be emplaced in a discernable pattern, and locating them near distinctive landmarks was to be avoided. However, it was a priority to locate them where they could fire on the key avenues of approach, and so sometimes they were emplaced in obvious locations. Trenches were not dug in angular geometric patterns, but followed contour lines, and even on flat ground they contained irregular twists and turns.

As noted previously, the layout and size of strongpoints varied greatly. Model diagrams depict them as oval shaped, but they could be very irregular in shape depending on the terrain. This necessary lack of uniformity was of a benefit to the defenders as it meant that attackers were confronted with many different layouts.

Most fortifications were built flush with the ground or kept as low as possible for concealment. Fortifications with embrasures by necessity had to be above ground level, but their profiles were also kept low. They featured banked earth on the sides, piled thick and angled steeply; despite being packed down, it was still sufficiently loose to absorb armour-piercing projectiles and the blast and fragmentation of HE. Bunkers with sufficiently thick roofs were often provided with a burster or protective layer laid just below the top. This comprised rocks, logs, or rubble. Sometimes a single layer of logs was laid atop the roof, but set flush with the roof's level as an outer burster layer.

The thickness of overhead cover was not always specified, but a minimum of 20–30cm of overhead soil cover was recommended for covered trenches in

Digging in

Riflemen were issued a small entrenching tool with a fixed square or pointed blade and a short wooden handle, 50cm long overall. Both types were carried in canvas carriers attached to the belt on the right hip. The Red Army used so many captured German entrenching tools that the folding shovel was discussed in the Soviet manual. Some members of rifle platoons carried small hatchets for cutting logs and stakes, clearing brush, and hacking out roots. Troop units were issued long-handle spades, pick-axes, axes, and hoes for constructing field fortifications. The use of these regularly sized tools sped up the work. Since there were often shortages of issued tools, civilian tools were confiscated and captured tools were valued. Wire cutters, handsaws,

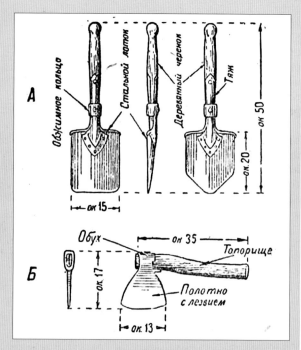

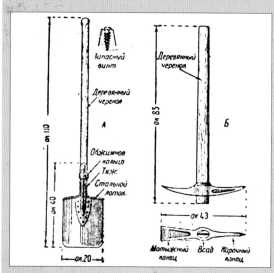

two-man crosscut saws, hammers, and malls (large wooden mallets for driving in posts and barbed-wire stakes) were also provided. Engineer troops used some two-man, petrol-powered chainsaws. Powered construction equipment suitable for building fortifications was almost unheard of. Most crawler-type tractor production served as artillery prime movers and in agriculture. What powered equipment was available was mostly dedicated to road and bridge repair/construction.

addition to the 10–14cm-diameter roofing logs. The roofs of other bunkers, shelters, and positions varied from 30–40cm and up to 1m. It was not uncommon for them to be much thicker. Waterproof roofing materials were extremely scarce. A 5–10cm layer of clay was sometimes laid over the logs for marginal protection from rain.

The logs used for above-ground sides of bunkers were 15cm and larger, with 20–30cm being preferred. They were often assembled log cabin style using top and bottom notches. Gaps between logs could be sealed by clay, mud mixed with straw or pine needles, or moss. Side logs were also stacked and held in place by driven-in vertical posts, inside and out.

German 5cm and 8cm mortar shells did not possess the weight to penetrate most bunkers. Their 12cm mortar, a copy of the Soviet HM-38, was much more effective. German 7.5cm infantry guns and 10.5cm howitzers had little effect as well. It required 15cm infantry guns and howitzers to have a significant effect, and a great deal of ammunition expenditure was needed. The Germans may have fielded more artillery in a division than the Soviets, but they were deficient in medium and heavy non-divisional artillery, having placed too much reliance on dive-bombers. The Nebelwefer multiple-rocket launchers, while generating a great deal of blast effect, were relatively inaccurate and created shallow craters.

Entrances to positions were normally in the rear, but in some instances they might be on the side, depending on the protection and concealment afforded by surrounding terrain. Entrances were often protected to prevent direct fire, blasts, shell fragments, grenades, and demolitions from entering. This might comprise a blast barrier inside the position or a similar barrier or wall on the outside. The entrance was often reached via a trench with at least one right-angle turn, though many positions had only a straight, unprotected entry trench. For attackers who gained the position's rear, this often proved to be a death trap, as they were usually protected by fire from adjacent positions.

Open trenches were to be covered with purpose-made, long, narrow camouflage nets, or wire mesh fencing. The net or mesh was then at least partly covered with appropriate ground-cover material, leaves, evergreen needles, or small tree limbs. Besides providing camouflage, these coverings prevented observers and aerial photograph interpreters from spying on Soviet troop activities. The nets and mesh were supposed to be sufficiently well anchored to prevent shell-blasted light debris from falling into the trench.

Emphasis was placed on providing an embrasure through trench parapets, rather than allowing for firing over the top alone. This could be a simple hand-dug slot, a sandbag-lined slot, or a slot with 6–8cm-thick logs or planks roofed over it and covered by a single layer of sandbags. The sides of embrasures were not lined with rocks, as bullets and rock splinters would ricochet into the firer. Designs were also provided for covered embrasures made entirely of planks, or small logs, or edged with logs and roofed with planks. In lieu of planks, logs split lengthwise were used. The side edging logs were to be 8–10cm in diameter, the recommended height of the embrasure's opening.

In weapons emplacements with overhead cover two embrasures were provided, either for two weapons, such as machine guns, or as an alternate embrasure to cover another part of the sector. The firing sector for the two embrasures overlapped to some degree. In concrete positions the openings of these ports were constructed in a 'stepped' manner, sometimes called a 'German embrasure'. This prevented bullets and fragments from ricocheting into the port. Embrasures were usually set at or just above ground level, and typically provided a 60-degree field of fire, which was the standard for concrete fortifications.

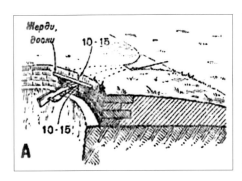

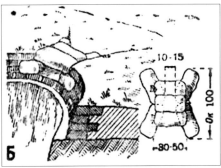

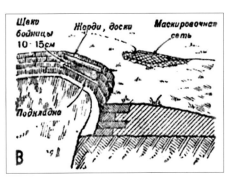

Three examples of firing embrasures for fighting positions and trenches: planks (top), sandbags supported by small logs (middle), and small logs and planks (bottom). Note that the opening on 'B' is concealed with an individual camouflage net. The embrasure's height was to be 10–15cm and its narrowest width the same. (Author's collection)

A trench parapet, plank-constructed firing embrasure manned by a PPSh-41-armed submachine gunner. Hand grenades were kept close by, as can be seen here. These include an F-1 fragmentation, three RGD-33 HE stick, and two RPG-40 anti-tank grenades. Soviet grenades were painted olive drab. (CMAF)

Limbs, saplings, and thick vines were woven horizontally wicker-style through 3cm vertical stakes at 40cm intervals as trench revetments. They were constructed in 3–4m-long sections. Horizontal planking was also used and supported by the same types of stakes, but with 10–14cm vertical stakes at 100–150cm intervals. Spreader struts helped prevent the revetting from collapsing. These were the same diameter as the vertical stakes and spanned the top ends of these. The vertical stakes could be reinforced by securing anchor wires to the tops and fastening them to short driven stakes driven 2.5–3m from the trench's edge just inside and under the edge of the parapet earth. Vertical planks were also used for revetting, a practice seldom seen elsewhere. These had pointed ends and were driven into the bottom of the trench to a depth of 25–30cm. The top ends were secured at the trench lip by long, horizontal, 5cm sapling poles held in place by staked wires under the parapet, in the same manner as the vertical stakes holding horizontal planks in place.

Combat experience showed that anti-tank gun firing positions needed to be carefully selected. Placing them under trees was to be avoided, as artillery and mortar rounds would air burst and shower the gun crew even if sheltered in slit trenches; nor were the guns to be positioned near prominent landmarks, as this made it easy for enemy observers to use such features as reference points to direct fire.

A tour of the fighting positions

The field fortifications described here are largely as prescribed in the 1942 Soviet manual *Infantry Fortifications*. Others are based on descriptions, originally from German sources, from the US Army's 1946 technical manual, *Handbook on USSR Military Forces*. Other examples are taken from various German wartime publications. The dimensions specified in manuals may seem precise, but in reality there was great variance.

Riflemen's positions

The most basic fighting position was the hasty rifleman's position, a skirmisher's pit. It was intended to provide a rifleman minimal protection and could be dug with an entrenching tool in 8–12 minutes, depending on the hardness of the soil and whether the soldier was kneeling or forced to lay prone under fire. Stones and roots would increase the time taken. The position consisted of a roughly 80cm-wide, 110–120cm-long, oval-shaped hole 20cm deep in the forward end and sloping upward to the rear. This barely provided cover for the soldier's torso and hips. His legs would be flat on the ground behind the hole. Spoil was piled in a 20cm-high, 80–90cm-thick crescent to the front, on which he laid his rifle for firing; there was no provision for a firing slot. The position, especially the parapet, was to be camouflaged with local vegetation. At the beginning of the war soldiers were issued 0.76 x 1.37m camouflage nets (to be garnished with vegetation), which could cover part of him and the position including the parapet. Such luxuries soon disappeared from the soldier's issue. Recognizing that the small parapet offered little real protection, an alternative design was provided. This specified two sandbags to be placed one in front of the other atop 5cm of spoil, and the rest of the spoil piled in a larger crescent beyond the front and ends of the sandbags for a 25–30cm-high parapet. The soldier carried the two already filled sandbags to the position. The hole could be 10–15cm deep. Its construction required 20–25 minutes, including pre-filling the sandbags.

Although not prescribed, soldiers often dug shallow, full body-length slit trenches for protection from shelling and bombing. Such positions were often dug as sleeping shelters behind the front.

A position offering more protection, and which the shallow hasty position could be expanded into, was a simple rectangular hole just large enough for a rifleman to kneel in. The Germans called this a 'Russian hole' (*russischloch* or *rusloch*). The hole was 80cm in width, 90–100cm in length, and 60–70cm deep, depending on the size of the man, and 70 x 70cm at the bottom. The frontal parapet was 30cm high and a little thicker. A 15–20cm lip was left between the hole and parapet as an elbow rest. This position required 25–30 minutes to dig. The corners of this and other positions were rounded rather than squared off.

The next step was to continue deepening and improving the position to a 90–110cm square hole with a depth of about 110cm, but adjustable to the soldier's height. It was 50–60cm across at the bottom. Besides depth the main improvement was an

(A) A section fighting trench with firing steps. The arrows indicate the direction of drainage flow if the trench is properly engineered.
(Б) A cross-section of the fighting trench with small drainage ditches dug along the bottom.
(В) A covered trench sump for drain-water. (Author's collection)

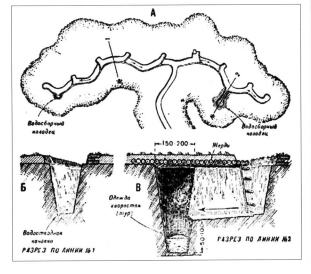

A crouching-type communications trench outside Leningrad. Note that in this instance the spoil has been thrown to the enemy side along at least part of the trench to provide a higher parapet. A 7.62mm DP-armed machine gunner is in the foreground. (Author's collection)

all-round parapet with a 15–20cm lip around the inside edge. The parapet was 30cm high and wider to the front and proportionally thinner to the sides and rear. This position provided sufficient spoil to build a parapet thick enough to protect from rifle and machine-gun fire. If built from the beginning as this type of position, as opposed to expanding it from the smaller positions, it was recommended that sod blocks be cut from where the hole was to be dug and used to reinforce the parapet's forward inside. This position required 50–60 minutes to construct. It was difficult for a soldier to squat deep into the bottom of this narrow hole for protection from over-running tanks. About 0.75m overhead clearance was necessary for protection from a tank's crushing action. This factor was incorporated into the designs of German and Western Allies fighting positions. No doubt soldiers learned to dig a roomier hole, allowing them to hide deeper.

The Soviets did not use two-man rifle positions, unlike US, Commonwealth, and German troops. They felt one-man positions could physically cover a wider platoon frontage, which was true to a degree. However, they sacrificed significant benefits. Two-man positions could cover just as wide a frontage as one-man positions with observation and fire. The standard interval between positions was 3–4m, but they were typically located at irregular intervals and the line staggered somewhat. Two-man foxholes allowed one man to dig while the other stood guard and took a break from digging. Once the position was completed one man slept and the other stood watch. If one man became a casualty the position was still manned and less of a gap was created. The second man could also provide first aid to his wounded comrade. A major benefit was the moral support a two-man position provided. There were instances when two individual positions were dug within a metre or so of one another and shared a common frontal parapet.

Another drawback of the design of these positions was that there was no accommodation for sleeping. While not addressed in manuals, because of the German use of air-burst artillery fire using mechanical time fuses, soldiers learned to dig a small niche into the bottom of their holes just large enough to squat in.

14.5mm anti-tank rifle positions often comprised whatever cover and concealment the two-man crew could find, as the true value of these weapons lay in their mobility. The weapons were heavy and awkward, but the barrel could be easily detached by the flip of a lever. The gunner carried the receiver group and the assistant the barrel.

A hasty two-man anti-tank rifle position was similar to the rifleman's. A single hole was dug with its rear sloping upward, but it was 1.60m wide to allow the assistant to lay to the gunner's right. With the bolt-action PTRD-41 the gunner opened the bolt ejecting the spent case and the assistant inserted the next round. The rifle was positioned and the crescent-shaped parapet, allowing for a 30cm lip, was thrown up burying the rifle's bipod with the rifle appearing to lie atop the 30cm-high parapet. The crew could complete the position in 10–15 minutes. A crescent-shaped AT rifle position provided a platform for the rifle on the inside of the crescent.

Machine-gun positions

A rifle battalion had a high density of machine guns, typically 48 light and heavy, and could be augmented by additional heavies from the division. A rifle platoon generally had six light machine guns with two in two of the sections and one in the other two. If armed with two guns they would be positioned in the section line with one near the end to cover the gap between the adjacent platoon and the other in the centre. If there were gaps between section strongpoints both guns might be positioned near the flanks. Single-gun sections usually located the weapon near the centre of the line. Regardless of this, machine guns would be positioned where they could best cover possible enemy infantry avenues of approach through areas offering cover and concealment. If fighting on open terrain they were placed to cover the section's front and/or exposed flanks and gaps. Machine guns figured in anti-tank defence in that they were important in separating dismounted infantry from tanks, to make them more vulnerable to shock group attack; the tanks were then fired on, to force them into closer formation.

The hasty light machine-gun position was essentially two adjacent riflemen's positions. The rifle-armed assistant gunner's position was within arm's reach (approximately 60cm), to enable him to hand magazines to the gunner, to the right of the gunner's hole and slightly to the rear. The forward edge of the assistant gunner's hole was aligned with the rear edge of the gunner's hole. The difference between the gunner's position and a rifleman's position was that the 20cm-high, crescent-shaped parapet was placed 100cm in front of the hole to allow room for the bipod-mounted weapon. With both men working it required 10–15 minutes to complete the position. The width of the field of fire from this type of position was limited and it could not effectively cover the section's entire front.

Light machine-gun equivalents of the two deeper riflemen's positions were also specified. As with the hasty position they consisted of two individual holes in roughly the same relation to each other as the hasty position. The machine-gunner's parapet was again 100cm forward. The full-depth position's parapet completely surrounded both holes. A two-man position was also prescribed in the form of a small semicircular trench with the inside of the curve providing a platform for the weapon. A short trench would connect the position to the

Members of a regimental submachine-gun company take up positions among steel hedgehog anti-tank obstacles. Armed with 7.62mm PPSh-41s, they may be members of an anti-tank shock group. In the defence submachine-gun units were employed as such, as well as a counter-attack force. (CMAF)

main trench to the rear. Internal dimensions were basically the same as the deep rifleman's position. A 50cm-wide firing slot was provided in the parapet, which entirely surrounded the position. Often planks or small-diameter logs would cover the slot and sod blocks or sandbags were stacked atop to protect the crew's heads.

On the edge of a trench the light machine-gun position was similar to a rifleman's one, but the parapet was placed 100cm forward of it. A firing slot was provided through the parapet. The position was usually the first to be covered when the trench was occupied for a prolonged period.

The SPM-10 Maxim heavy machine-gun positions were more elaborate. The Maxim was mounted on a two-wheel carriage with a shield. The shield offered little protection from all but long-range rifle fire, but did provide some protection from fragments. The hasty position comprised two shallow scraped holes, like the rifleman's, with the assistant gunner's to the right and just forward of the gunner's by half its length. The roughly 30cm-wide area between the holes was scraped out with a combined width of approximately 160cm. The spoil was piled 20cm high in an irregular crescent to the front and sides. A 70cm-wide, 140cm-long, ground-level platform was provided in front of the gunner's hole for the weapon. The SG-43 machine gun, which never completely replaced the Maxim, used the same emplacement and was also mounted on a two-wheel carriage with a shield. However, the quantity of soil dug from the two holes and the narrow connecting scarp were insufficient for the parapet size depicted in the plan. The gunner and his assistant could dig the position in 10–15 minutes. The rest of the crew would dig riflemen's positions to the flanks where they held additional ammunition containers and provided protection.

A machine-gun position that provided more cover and allowed the crew to kneel down consisted of an L-shaped trench. The 'arm' for the gunner was 120cm long on the inside, and the base of the 'L' for the assistant to the right was 100cm long on the inside. The 60–70cm-deep trench was 90cm across the top and 60–70cm wide at the bottom. The machine gun sat on the ground-level platform formed around the 'L'. A 70cm niche in the parapet for the gun and a 140cm-long platform were provided. The 25cm-high parapet wrapped around the front and part of the sides. This same position was also used for a 50mm mortar, which was typically employed as a line-of-sight weapon.

For a deeper position the back width of the 'L' trench was dug out to provide space to set the machine gun in the bottom; this helped to protect the weapon from shell fragments. The trench was deepened to 100–110cm, resulting in it measuring 40–50cm across the bottom. The parapet was heightened to 30cm and extended further around the sides and behind the gunner. The position could be built in 1 hour 45 minutes. Such a position could be covered with a sufficiently supported 15–17cm-diameter log roof and topped with earth. A wood-frame or log embrasure was usually provided. Several more elaborate plans were given for roofed machine-gun bunkers. These were usually incorporated into trench systems and strongpoints. One plan provided for a wooden firing platform, topped by a layer or two of sandbags, underneath which the machine gun could be sheltered.

An appendage to the position was a narrow extension of the left end of the L-shaped trench, which ran for 4–5m and curved around to the front left. An observer's position was situated in the trench's end with a vision slot to the

A covered machine-gun position

This bunker houses a 7.62mm Maxim SPM-10 machine gun, and is constructed of 20cm-diameter side wall logs and roofed over with 15cm-diameter logs. The roof is capped with 5cm of clay for waterproofing and 30cm of soil. The crew pit is revetted by planks held in place with stakes. The rear entry trench connects the bunker to the main fighting trench. The plank embrasure to the right is similar to those made for riflemen's trench positions. Camouflage has not yet been added to this bunker. A plan view is shown in the bottom left.

A covered machine-gun position

front. This allowed the section leader to be positioned sufficiently to the side, where he would not draw fire, and be provided a clear view free from the machine-gun's smoke and dust for observing and correcting fire. The extension trench's spoil provided a parapet on both sides and additional spoil for more protection behind the gun. The extension and other improvements to the position could be completed in 1 hour 30 minutes. In positions without this extension trench the section leader's hole was located to the flank.

A square of canvas or a split-open sandbag could be pegged down on the forward slope of the parapet and camouflaged with small limbs. This reduced muzzle-blast dust, which could reveal the position. An ammunition niche could be dug in the forward end of the assistant gunner's trench at the bottom of the 'L'.

Plans for anti-aircraft machine-gun positions for the Maxim machine gun M1931 quad mount, the 12.7mm DShK-39, or a single Maxim on an anti-aircraft tripod were available. For the single Maxim the circular pit was approximately 240cm in diameter at the top and 200cm at the bottom. It was 115cm deep and surrounded by a wide, 20cm-high parapet. This allowed the gun to engage ground targets. The gun was not set up in the pit's centre, but to the forward side to allow space for the gunner. This prevented 360-degree fire, which would have required a much wider pit and considerably more digging time. With the entire crew digging, the pit and trench could be prepared in 1 hour 15 minutes. The 12.7mm pit was about 60cm larger in diameter. The quad Maxim mount required an even larger pit and the gun was mounted in the centre. The mount consisted of a large, steel, cone-shaped pedestal, which was bolted to a heavy timber platform.

An expedient AA mounting was a circular pit with a 20–25cm-diameter, 1.2–1.3m-high post solidly planted in it. A wooden wagon wheel was mounted onto the post, and a Maxim was fitted to this. A 150cm-deep trench ran from the pit to one side as a protective shelter, or to connect the position to a communications trench linking other positions. A short ramp gave acccess from the shallower pit into the trench. A 70 x 70cm ammunition niche was dug in the side of the pit, or the trench, or both.

A specialized type of light machine-gun position was sometimes built in the angle of anti-tank ditches (see the illustration on page 10). This would be built as small as possible, with a very small, 35-degree embrasure oriented to cover one leg of the ditch; the latter was for engaging infantry seeking cover and clearing wire and mines. It was just large enough for the two-man crew and protected them from grenades. If possible it was connected to the main defensive position by a covered or open trench. This served as an entry and escape route, but the defenders of this position would probably consider it their grave; the position was down in a ditch and they were blind to everything going on around them other than what was happening in their field of fire along the ditch. To protect these positions from surface attack rifle positions were dug to cover them. Machine guns could also cover the ditch positions. Barbed wire was placed on the forward edge of the ditches some 40m from the angle-covering positions, to keep enemy infantry out of grenade range. Anti-tank rifles and guns were sometimes emplaced at the angles, and even submachine guns and rifles were used if there were insufficient machine guns.

Mortar and anti-tank gun positions

Mortars were often set up behind any available cover, including in gullies, draws, on hillocks, in sunken road sections, and behind embankments, walls, rubble piles, log cabins, and other low structures. When such positions were built they were usually only large enough for the mortar and could only be oriented in the primary direction of fire. A considerably larger pit was required to allow 360-degree fire, which was sometimes necessary in strongpoints. Such positions were just large enough for the gunner and his assistant. A major

A battalion mortar platoon digs in, a major effort considering the amount of earth that had to be moved to complete the positions. Once the digging was completed the parapets would be camouflaged. The three positions are 3–4m apart. The mortars are 82mm PM-43s with integral transport wheels on the bipods, which could be removed once positioned. Note the handle fitting on the muzzles, allowing it to be pulled by one or two men. (RGAKFD)

prerequisite for selecting mortar positions was overhead clearance, that is, without obstructing trees and telephone/power lines.

For the 82mm mortar an oval-shaped pit was dug 200cm long from side to side, 170–80cm wide front to rear, and 150cm across the bottom. A small, angled depression was dug into the back edge of the pit's bottom and slightly into the back wall for the oval base plate. The repeated recoil on the mortar base plates pounded them deeper into the ground, even in firm soil, and so in areas of soft soil short logs or sandbags were laid horizontally below the base plate; sometimes small rocks might be placed beneath sandbags. The pit was surrounded by a wide, 30cm-high parapet.

On either end of the oval pit a short trench was dug to accommodate one man. This was a stepped hole with the first step 110cm deep and the bottom one 150cm deep. The gunner was to the mortar's left and the assistant to the right. If connected to a communications trench it would run out one of the ends via the man hole. An ammunition niche was placed in the side of the trench.

A larger 82mm mortar position was similar, but comprised a circular pit 240cm in diameter, allowing the base plate to be positioned in the centre for all-round fire. The 120mm mortar pit was 340cm across. Because of their size and the requirement that mortar positions be placed in the open for firing clearance, they were difficult to conceal.

45mm anti-tank gun positions were 30cm-deep, 4m-diameter pits surrounded by low parapets. A 4m-long slit trench was dug to one side as a crew shelter. It included an ammunition niche and could be covered by logs and earth. On the other side a 5.5m-long, 2m-wide inclined trench was dug for the gun to be rolled into, for protection from artillery. It, too, could be roofed over. A 57mm gun pit was roughly one metre wider in diameter. 76mm field guns could be emplaced in similar positions since they had a secondary anti-tank role. When emplaced in normal artillery positions they were still sited to enable them to engage tanks.

The firing position would ideally be provided with overhead cover, in order to protect anti-tank weapons and at the same time to retain their ability to provide all-round fire. This was seldom possible and most anti-tank guns appeared in open-topped

An 82mm mortar position. An improved position of similar design had a circular pit 2.40m in diameter with the mortar in the centre. Here the gunner and his assistant are provided with stepped holes in which to shelter when receiving artillery fire. Note the ammunition niche in the connecting trench. (Author's collection)

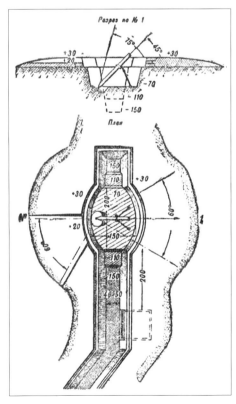

An anti-tank gun position

An anti-tank gun position

This fully developed 45mm M-1937 anti-tank gun position was the same as that used for 37mm and 57mm anti-tank guns. 76mm field guns in an anti-tank role would also use this type of position. Its design allowed all-round fire, a key requirement when emplacing anti-tank guns. The position's design required a low parapet and overhead cover on the adjacent shelters. The gun could be rolled into a shelter when under fire, where complete protection was provided for the crew. Normally a position would be well camouflaged, but this has been removed here for clarity; a plan view of the position is also shown in the bottom left. Anti-tank gun platoons consisted of two guns, and the two positions would be within 50m of each other, covering the same sector of fire. Ideally the two guns would engage the same tank, but if a large number of tanks were within range they would engage different ones. Often anti-tank gun positions were simple pits with only crew slit trenches to the sides, and used only the natural cover available.

positions. Provision was made for rifle and machine-gun positions around an anti-tank gun position, for close-in protection. Crew dugouts, ammunition niches, and communications trenches were also provided. Dugouts and shelters of reserve ammunition and equipment were 10–20m to the rear of crew-served weapons-firing positions.

Trenches

The Soviets tended to use trenches more widely, particularly within strongpoints, than other nations in World War II. Trench width at the top and bottom varied, depending on their depth, as the sides were gradually sloping. Wide parapets of equal width were raised on both sides, 30–40cm high. Regardless of any specified trench width, consideration was given to the need to pull a Maxim machine gun on its wheeled carriage through a trench. This required a minimum bottom width of 70cm. Wider trenches also aided the passage of litter bearers carrying wounded. The Soviets, like most period armies, had generally eliminated angular and geometrical patterns, which were easily detectable from the air and required additional effort to lay out. Instead, trenches followed natural terrain contours

An 82mm mortar position. It is revetted with vertical planks held in place by log stakes. The trench to the rear connects to ammunition niches and a crew shelter. The position has been dug behind a small knoll. (CMAF)

Troops employ a captured German 7.5cm Pak.40 anti-tank gun. The position is partly revetted with logs, and is poorly camouflaged. Similar positions would be used for other anti-tank guns and the 76mm F-22 field gun. (RGAKFD)

and vegetation lines to blend them in. A snaking contour was useful if a trench section was hit, as the blast and fragmentation could easily travel through a lengthy straight section.

Parapets were to be concealed using replaced ground cover or cut limbs. Camouflage nets or wire mesh were stretched over the trench and pinned down with stakes. The nets/mesh at least partly covered the parapet. Longer tree limbs were also placed over trenches, and lattice works of long reeds and twigs were also used to support camouflage. Trenches were frequently constructed within built-up areas to connect defended buildings and strongpoints. Such trenches twisted their way through mounds of rubble, and might be reinforced with broken concrete, paving slabs, masonry, planks, and timbers. The latter were also used to cover trenches, with rubble scattered over them as camouflage.

Four standardized sizes of trenches were specified. In practice, they were naturally varied according to the trench's purpose, hardness of soil, construction time, and proximity to the front. These trenches included the 'crawling' type – a shallow trench relying on its parapets for sufficient depth to protect a soldier crawling on his belly. The 'stooping' type allowed the soldier to move bent over

This 45mm M-1937 anti-tank gun position has been dug somewhat deeper than was normal. The parapet has been well camouflaged with grass and small branches. Note that the pit's floor has been camouflaged from aerial observation. The ascending cloud of muzzle smoke demonstrates one of the difficulties of concealing an anti-tank gun position. (CMAF)

This artillery battery commander's observation post is roofed with logs and topped with rocks and camouflaging brush. A tripod-mounted, BST, scissors-type battery commander scope was standard equipment. (CMAF)

or on all fours. The 'full-height' type allowed a man to walk upright in it even with a camouflage net/mesh overhead; it, too, relied on parapets. The full-height type with overhead cover was deeper and was not constructed with a parapet, but with 2m-long, 10–14cm-diameter logs or planks laid crossways on ground-level stringer supports 20cm from the lip. The spoil was spread over the cover 20–30cm thick, and the position camouflaged.

Table 3: Trench dimensions (in cm)

Type	Top width	Bottom width	Depth	Parapet height
Crawling	80–90	70–75	60	30
Stooping	90–100	60	110	30
Full-height	100–110	40	150	40
Covered	120	50	180	0

Any of these trenches could be used as firing trenches by digging firing steps in the sides and cutting firing slots through the parapet. Trenches, especially communications ones, could be completely covered for their entire length. Fighting trenches might be partly covered, ideally in 3–4m sections with approximately a 1.5m gap between each. This allowed soldiers to emerge and observe or throw grenades. Trenches were seldom covered to this extent, though.

In wet areas, during periods of heavy rain and snowmelt, duckboards made of small logs or planks were installed in the bottom of trenches over drainage

PAGE 42 ILLUSTRATION
The construction of a section trench
A section trench system was built in five stages, over the course of 4–5 days.

Stage 1: individual fighting positions were prepared approximately 3–4m apart with the two-man light machine-gun (LMG) position in the centre (marked with large red arrows here).

Stages 2 and 3: the fighting positions were improved and connected by a crawl trench, with each man working towards the LMG. Stage 3 saw the trench deepened, an exit trench prepared, and 'reserve firing positions' created to engage targets to the rear or flanks.

Stage 4: the firing positions were further improved with covered embrasures, ammunition niches were dug, and reserve firing positions were prepared in the ends of the trench and along the communications trench. The latter ran to the rear to connect to trenches that linked the platoon's other sections.

Stage 5: dugouts were prepared in the forward trench, trench sections were covered, drainage sumps were added, a 4–5m extension was added to the shelter trench and covered (note escape exit), and other refinements were made throughout. Some 30–50m to the rear (shown nearer here) a 4–5m-long slit trench was dug off the communications trench.

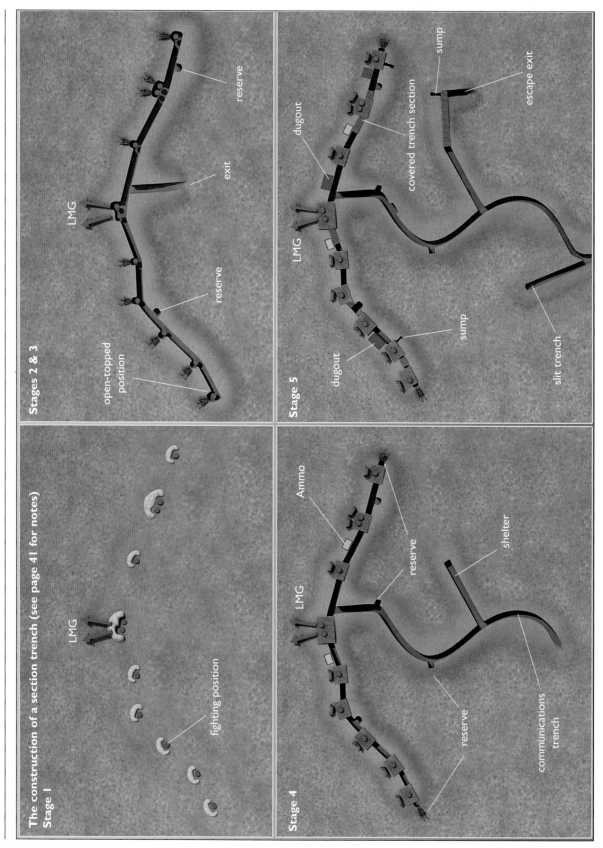

The construction of a section trench (see page 41 for notes)

Stage 1

LMG

fighting position

Stages 2 & 3

LMG

exit

reserve

reserve

open-topped position

Stage 4

LMG

Ammo

reserve

reserve

shelter

communications trench

Stage 5

LMG

dugout

dugout

sump

sump

covered trench section

escape exit

slit trench

42

Completed and improved section trench (see page 44 for notes)

Section view of LMG position

Covered firing embrasure

Completed and improved section trench

The completely developed section trench system often included short trench extensions dug forward from the main trench. Ammunition niches would be dug into the sides of some of these. The section trench could be linked to other section trenches within the platoon via communications trenches in the rear, or the section's forward trenches could be linked end-to-end. If time and materials were available more trench sections would be covered or camouflage nets/mesh erected over all sections. Barbed-wire obstacles would be some 40m forward, outside of hand-grenade range. The lower left inset shows a covered firing embrasure. The centre right inset shows a section view of the LMG bunker.

ditches. To keep water from washing away rear parapets and flowing into the trenches down the sides, small barrier ditches were dug uphill several metres behind the trench and running parallel with it.

Troop bunkers and shelters

Soldiers needed protection both from artillery and mortar fire, and the weather. Sheltered positions, featuring thick overhead cover, varied from one-man dugouts to section and larger versions. These shelters were built near fighting positions, command and observation posts, and throughout the rear area for support and service troops. They were to be placed 30–60m from large, crew-served weapons positions to keep them clear of any counter-battery fire.

The most basic shelter was a one-man dugout, a simple niche dug into the forward side of a trench. This dugout was cut with the long axis parallel with the trench rather than perpendicular to it; a perpendicular-cut dugout offered more protection, but required much more time to dig and was extremely difficult to do because of the narrow working space. The dugout was 160–180cm in length, 60cm wide (i.e. deep into the trench's side), and 60–80cm high. Rather than squaring it off, the corners and ceiling were rounded. It permitted a man to lie down lengthwise, with his weapon and equipment beside him. The Soviet manual depicts the dugout's bottom level with the trench floor, but soldiers learned to dig it 15cm or more above the trench's bottom to prevent flooding. A soldier might peg his rain cape over the opening in rainy or cold weather.

A more sophisticated dugout used notched planks assembled into 100 x 100cm frames. The 5cm-thick, 18–28cm-wide planks had interlocking notches on the ends to allow them to be assembled. The soldier dug a square hole 100–120cm deep into the side of the trench, slightly larger than the assembled frames, and inserted them one behind the other as he progressed inward. Any gaps outside the frames were backfilled with loose dirt. This required 4–8 frames, depending on the dugout's depth and the width of the frames. Once the frames were inserted, diagonal braces were nailed to the sides and the back wall planked over. A soldier

BELOW LEFT A simple, one-man dugout cut into the side of a fighting trench. It provided some degree of protection from shellfire and the weather, plus kept the trench clear for movement. Note the brick-like stacking of the sod blocks in the forward parapet. (Author's collection)

BELOW RIGHT A more elaborate dugout constructed with notched-end planks. The back wall has been planked, diagonal braces fitted (essential), a sill board added to keep out water, and plank entrance cover provided. This was useful in rainy or cold weather. (Author's collection)

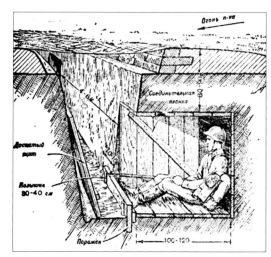

could sit inside this, but one in which he could lie down required a 180–200cm-deep hole and 6–8 hours to construct. These dugouts were to be 4–6m apart.

A multi-man dugout was dug into trench sides to accommodate 3–5 men. This was a cut-and-cover shelter. A 3m-wide area was dug down to 50–60cm depth. This would be 2–3m long perpendicular to the trench, depending on the number of men it would shelter. Stringer logs were laid near the 170cm-wide edges of the pit. 3m-long, 15–17cm-diameter logs were laid over these for the roof. This was topped with two layers of sandbags, if available, and earth to ground level. Often, more earth would be heaped on top for a thicker roof. Two or three layers of crisscrossed logs might be used too. The shelter itself was then dug out from the trench side underneath the log roof. An earth bench seat was left on one side roughly level with the trench floor and a narrow slit trench dug in front of the seat for leg space. This, of course, was the hard way to do it, but protected the diggers working from inside the trench. It required 4–5 hours' work. If enemy fire was not a concern, the pit could be dug faster from above before laying the roofing logs.

A T-34 tank parked in a hiding pit. This would be covered over with tree branches and the tread marks swept away. This type of pit was strictly for concealment and the AFV was not meant to fire from it. (US Army)

This same type of dugout could be constructed in rear areas merely by digging it down into the ground and to the necessary length. Roofing logs were laid flat on the ground and the spoil heaped on the roof. Entry was through a small slit trench at one end or a simple manhole.

Another rear-area shelter was prepared on reverse slopes. An open-sided trench or shelf was cut into the slope, roofed over with long logs, and covered with spoil. Entry was through narrow slit trenches at one or both ends. A drainage diversion trench was dug above the shelter. This was an easy shelter for rear service troops to build.

For sections and larger groups, underground shelters were dug and buried completely below ground level. These were long slit trenches 100cm wide and providing 180–200cm floor-to-ceiling clearance. They were to have 30–40cm of cover above them, but again, in reality they had much thicker roofs featuring layers of criss-crossed logs, sandbags, rocks, and earth to protect them from artillery fire. Their length depended on the number of men to be housed. Earth seat platforms might be left along one wall, or plank/log benches used. There was an entrance trench or tunnel on both ends set at 90-degree angles. These types of bunkers could be used as chemical defence shelters by adding two sets of sealed doors to create 'airlock' chambers. A hand-operated air filter and air intake pipe were installed.

Living shelters were frequently built for four or six men, some 2–3m each side. They could be larger, containing a whole section, and might be subdivided into 'rooms' with blanket curtains. These were built along the lines of partly or completely buried log cabins (isba), often with a pecked roof of split logs. The roof might be covered with a layer of clay, sod, and thick layers of insulating evergreen boughs, with more sod or earth on top. If near the frontline they would have flat roofs protected by a thick mound of soil. A wood-fired stove might even be available. If not the occupants relied on candles and body heat for some minimal warmth. Two-tier plank bunks were sometimes built, or the earthen floors were covered with straw or evergreen boughs where men could sleep rolled up in their overcoats and, if fortunate, a blanket. Straw and boughs were used for padding and insulating plank bunks too.

Such shelters were used for winter quarters and were based on the traditional *zemlyanki* (pit houses dug into the ground built by serfs in treeless areas). They were covered with wagon planks, what logs they could obtain, and sods of earth. The soldier's *zemlyanki* were typically poorly ventilated, gloomy, cold, damp, musty, and smelt of wet wool, *makhorka* (poor-grade tobacco), food, and body odours. Some were fortunate enough to have a stove inside, and in these cases wood-cutting details were necessary. A soldier would have to stand fire guard if it burned through the night, and a sentry was always posted outside for one- or two-hour watches.

Camouflage techniques

Once they had begun to recover from the initial setbacks, the Red Army allotted much time to camouflage training, and also relied on both ingenuity and strict camouflage discipline. Many of the techniques the Soviets employed were new to the Germans. The following is a translation of a German pamphlet dated 1943 on Soviet summer camouflage.

Preface

The following examples were taken from reports from the front and captured orders. They represent only a part of Russian camouflage methods, but are in some cases new and worthy of imitation. They can be used in improved form by our own troops. A detailed knowledge of Russian camouflage methods helps our own troops recognize the enemy and his tricks without delay. In this way surprise is avoided and troops can operate with greater confidence.

Camouflage materials

The camouflage instinct is strongly developed in the Russian and his inventiveness is astounding. This system is systemically encouraged by thorough training beginning on the first day of training and is continued throughout the whole process. Camouflage discipline is good even among troops who otherwise might be well below the average in regard to weapons training. Violations of camouflage discipline are severely punished.

Prepared camouflage materials

[The phrases below such as 'different/various coloured/shades' refer to various green and brown shades.]

Summer camouflage suit: the suit consists of a jacket and hood of coloured material in which tufts of matting in various shades are woven. In appropriate surroundings, a man in a prone position in his clothing cannot be seen more than a few paces away. There is also a brown suit printed with black splotches.

Summer camouflage smock: this consists of coloured material with patches in dark shades and is suitable for use against a broken background of woods and bushes.

Camouflage net for riflemen: the net is about 0.75 x 1.5m and weighs about 0.33kg. It is garnished with natural camouflage materials from the immediate surroundings and can be used either as a covering or spread out in front of the rifleman. By binding several nets together rifle and machine gun positions and entrances to dugouts can be camouflaged.

Camouflage screen for riflemen: this consists of a wire contraption divided into several pieces that open fan-like, covered with material. In it is a hole through which a rifle can protrude. It represents a bush and is provided in three different colours. It can be folded up and carried on the person in a bag. The rifleman lies in such a position behind the screen that his body is hidden. In the attack he can crawl forward and push the screen before him. The screen is only visible to the naked eye at a range of 150–200 paces.

Camouflage cover for machine gun: the cover consists of coloured fabric in which tufts of coloured matting are woven. When moving forward the cover will not be removed. The machine gun with this cover can only be recognized when within 100m.

Camouflage fringe: the fringe consists of a band about 3m long from which grass-coloured matting is hung. On the ends are hooks for attaching the fringe on the equipment to be hidden. A rifleman can fix the fringe on the helmet or shoulders. Five of these fringes are used to camouflage a machine gun and six for an anti-tank gun.

Camouflage nets: for covering gun positions or trenches nets of various sizes are issued. The net is woven with pieces of coloured fabric or paper. When in use additional natural camouflage is added such as grass, twigs, etc. These nets are also used by tanks, tractors, trucks, and trailers. The standard net is about 4m square, and by joining several together, large surfaces can be camouflaged against aerial observation.

Camouflage carpet: this consists of strips of various sizes into which coloured matting and tufts are woven. It is used mostly for camouflaging earthworks.

Improvised camouflage materials

Observation and sniping posts: a tree stump is hollowed out and stakes are used as supports. Another method is to insert a periscope into a frame made to look like a wooden cross in cemeteries. Imitation hayricks are often used.

Camouflage against observation from the air: shadows can be cast by fixing frameworks on the side of a house or on the roof so that by distorting its form the object cannot be recognized. Branches fixed on wire strung over the object can make it invisible from the air.

Camouflaging tanks and tank tracks: when being transported by rail or when on the road, tanks can be made to look like boxcars or ordinary trucks.

When there are groups of trees, camouflage can be quickly obtained by bending the tops of trees over objects to be camouflaged. Nets can also be spread over and attached to trees with natural camouflage laid on top. Among low bushes tanks can be made invisible by covers and even without natural camouflage nets or covers can completely alter the shape of tanks.

Tank tracks can be obscured by dragging fir tree limbs behind the tank. Rolls of barbed wire with an iron rod through them can also be used for this purpose.

Use of camouflage

On the march: as equipment being transported by rail cannot be fully concealed, the Russians attach particular importance to preventing the recognition of the type of equipment by making guns, vehicles, tanks, fuel trucks, etc. look like ordinary roofed freight cars. This is done by means of some sort of superstructure. Loading and unloading generally takes place at night, often in open country.

Fig. I

Fig. 2

Fig I: a 76mm M-1927/39 regimental gun camouflaged with nets over a ravine.
Fig. 2: an observation post in a cemetery with a periscope camouflaged as a cross.

Movement of large Russian units takes place either at night, with meticulous attention being paid to blackout regulations, or by day in wooded country. If the march must take place by day in country that offers only limited natural concealment, movement takes place by stages from cover to cover. Motor vehicles, where present, are diverted from main roads to side or forest roads. The bunching of vehicles at bridges, defiles, etc. is avoided. A group of vehicles will halt under cover some distance from a defile; the movement through the defile will be made only by single vehicles or in small groups.

On the approach of German aircraft, all vehicles take cover without delay. If single vehicles are forced to remain on the road, they either remain stationary, or, lacking any camouflage protection, take up positions diagonally on the road in order to look like broken-down vehicles.

Track discipline is carefully carried out. When tanks have to leave the main road they travel in single column as far as possible, in order not to give away their numbers by leaving individual sets of tracks.

Quarters and bivouacs

All evidence of the occupation of a village is avoided. Tanks, guns, and vehicles, if they cannot be brought under cover, are placed in irregular formations and camouflaged in yards and gardens, and against hedges, bushes, walls, and trees.

Special care is taken to see that movement from one place to another is limited to small groups; this rule applies also when issuing rations, fuel, etc.

Destroyed villages and burned-down premises are preferred for quartering men, weapons, equipment, and vehicles as these areas lend themselves easily to camouflage.

Bivouacs are cleverly camouflaged against houses, hedges, gardens, etc. If possible, thick woods are used, and use is made of branches to cover equipment. In open country, hollows and ditches are used to the utmost, and bivouacs spread out in irregular formations. Tents are covered with natural camouflage material; if this is lacking, tents are not used. Instead holes and pits are constructed. When bivouacs are taken up, tracks are obliterated in order to give the enemy no indication as to strength.

In battle

Stress is laid on the necessity of being able to crawl for long distances at a quick rate. Patrols are well equipped with camouflage suits, and make full use of darkness and poor visibility.

When working forward, the Russian moves in short, quick bounds, and is capable of moving through the thickest undergrowth in order to work his way close to German positions. If the defence is on the alert, he is able to lie still for hours on end.

Russian tree snipers are particularly difficult to detect. Tank-destroying sections with incendiary bottles, grenades, and mines are distributed in wheat fields and at places metres from the edges of woods and fields.

In defending built-up areas the Russians make use of positions outside the area. These consist of many rifle pits, organized in depth and well camouflaged along fences and brush. When firing from houses, machine guns are placed well back from windows and doorways to prevent the flash being seen, and also to smother the report.

When German aircraft appear all movement ceases.

After firing, any discolouration [burnt powder] in front of guns is covered with suitable camouflage material. When a gun remains for some time in one position, planks of sufficient size, painted to match the surroundings, can be laid in front of the muzzle.

As the presence of tanks leads to definite conclusions regarding the main effort of the attack, the Russians are very careful to camouflage their armour.

Layout of the defensive position

Reconnaissance patrols [i.e those reconnoitering future defensive positions] are instructed not only to study the ground from the tactical point of view, but also in regards to possibilities for camouflage. This includes the shape of ground formations, the background, colouring, available natural camouflage, and what suitable artificial camouflage material can be used. Positions are selected to conform to the natural contours of the ground, and comfort is of secondary importance. As much use as possible is made of reverse-slope positions. Parapets are kept as low as possible and are carefully camouflaged with grass, leaves, etc. Positions are often camouflaged with covers made of boards, fir branches, or straw. If time does not allow complete trenches to be dug, sections between individual positions will be covered so that to an observer they look like connected trenches. Provision is made to conceal vision slits. Anti-tank ditches are entirely or partially covered in such a way that they look like narrow, easily passable trenches. Pillboxes are carefully camouflaged with nets or covers. Exposed walls are painted with a mixture of tar and asphalt and then a layer or earth or straw. Wire obstacles can be made invisible by sighting them among hedges and fences.

In forests, thick undergrowth is preferred in selecting a position. Cutting down trees to give fields of fire is avoided for reasons of camouflage.

Russian signalmen use telegraph poles, with the bark still on, and set them up at irregular intervals. The line of poles is set to conform to the lie of the country. Spoil at

Fig. 3

Fig. 4

Fig. 3: wires strung between trestles and covered with branches screen a road from aerial observation.
Fig. 4: wires are used to bend trees over a parked T-27 light tank.

the foot of the poles is carefully camouflaged and trampling of the earth along the line of the piles is strictly avoided. Telephone wire is also laid to conform to the contour.

Camouflage discipline in occupied positions is very good, and one seldom hears talking, rattling of weapons, or sees the glimmer of a cigarette. In order to prevent the enemy realizing that a position is weakly held, single riflemen keep up strong fire activity at various points.

Dummy positions

Dummy trenches are of normal width, but are dug only to a depth of 0.5m. The bottom can be made dark by soot or pine needles. Dummy dugouts can be made by the use of props, with the entrance made of cardboard or paper painted black. Dummy loopholes or observation slits can be made out of black paper or felt. Dummy gun positions can be arranged by turning over grass or burning it in order to imitate discolouration from muzzle blast. Dummy gun positions must be located at correct intervals. The representation of dummy tracks leading to the dummy positions must not be forgotten. The desired result is achieved by mowing grass with a sickle, to the normal width of a track, and letting the cut grass remain, or rolling it with short logs. When the ground is open, colouration must be used in order to make the tracks light and the position dark.

Dummy obstacles can be erected by cutting grass and making small heaps out of the cuttings. In a ploughed field, it is sufficient to plough at right angles to the furrows, to the width of the particular obstacle it is desired to represent. Dummy mine pits can be made by taking sod blocks and laying them to the sides clumsily. The dummy minefields should be 2–4 times as obvious as normal minefields. In dummy minefields 5–10 percent of real mines are generally laid. Dummy light installations are used a great deal in order to portray a station, industrial plant, or airfield. Lanterns, dummy bivouacs, empty tents, dummy shelters, and campfires are often arranged to give the·impression of the presence of troops.

The test of battle

Developing a company strongpoint

A company strongpoint is examined here to illustrate how a typical strongpoint was constructed. It could be decentralized, as depicted here, or integrated into a battalion strongpoint. This particular company has been augmented by 45mm anti-tank gun, anti-tank rifle, 82mm mortar, and heavy machine gun platoons, plus a sapper section from the battalion and regiment; and has three rifle sections per platoon rather than four. The strongpoint is built on a low knoll with a deep ravine on its right flank, which has been incorporated into the obstacle plan, as has dense vegetation. It occupies an area about 300m across and 200m deep (see the illustration on page 52).

The company strongpoint comprised three platoon strongpoints, two covering the front and part of the flanks and the third providing a second line and covering a flank. The gaps to the flanks between adjacent company strongpoints were covered by weapons from both companies, as well as regimental guns and mortars, and divisional artillery.

The position for each company strongpoint was usually selected by the regiment. Regimental and battalion officers would survey the site and lay it out with marker stakes. The battalion and regiment would also dictate the positioning and sectors of fire of many of the crew-served weapons. It was essential that this be accomplished at these echelons to ensure fire was integrated with adjacent strongpoints and that gaps were covered. Even at company level the positioning of its platoons' light machine guns would be specified. Officers would survey the strongpoints and determine the amounts of construction and obstacle material needed, and coordinate its delivery from division and army engineer dumps. At regimental level simple construction lines might be set up to produce pre-fabricated building items. Advisors from the regimental engineer company would assist the battalion commanders. The first two days would largely be taken up with the use of infantry hand tools. Tools from regimental level were issued to crew-served weapons crews; after they had completed their positions these tools would be turned over to the infantry to expand and improve their positions.

It required at least six days to adequately prepare a strongpoint. The first step was the construction of section positions. At the same time command posts, crew-served weapons positions, and support facilities were prepared, along with obstacles and camouflage. Outposts were emplaced and security patrols conducted. Even if all defences and obstacles were completed, work continued on reinforced quarters, supply shelters, and further obstacles. The unit would make improvements right up to the moment the Germans attacked.

While construction was under way, wire communications were laid out from the higher unit to the lower – for example, battalion wire parties laid wire to its companies. The Red Army was well equipped with field telephones, switch-boards, and supporting gear. Wire teams laid field telephone wire through ditches, gullies, streambeds, and buried it if necessary for protection from artillery and mortar fire, as well as from friendly vehicle traffic. Wire was the primary means of communication in the defence, though radios might be used by outposts and artillery forward observers, who also had wire. Telephone lines were usually run down to platoon level. Within platoons, and sometimes within companies, voice and messengers were the main means of communications. Coloured flares fired from 26.5mm pistols were used to signal specific actions. Frontline positions were marked so friendly aircraft would not attack them with 1 x 3m white (summer) and red (winter) panels. Two double-sided panels were issued per platoon.

A T-34/76 tank is emplaced in a hull-defilade pit, which would enable it to fire. Across the road another tank is partly dug in under a shed. The tanks have been winter whitewashed. Note the German 7.9mm Kar.98k carbine in a handy position to take potshots at targets of opportunity. (CMAF)

The standard practice for the development of a section position was for its nine men to dig individual fighting holes 3–4m apart in an irregular pattern with the light machine gun in the centre. These would be connected by a crawl trench to their immediate rear, making the firing holes now firing steps in the forward side of the trench. The trench would be deepened, ammunition niches added in the forward trench wall, and a short exit trench dug to the rear near the centre. The firing slots would be converted to covered embrasures and a long curving communications trench dug rearward and connected to other trenches interlinking the platoon's sections. Often, and this was the preferred method, the 2–4m curving trenches were dug forward from each firing position and a new firing position prepared there. This greatly improved the ability to survive hits from heavy artillery. Some 30–50m to the rear of the main forward trench a 4–5m long protective trench was dug branching out of the side of the communications trench. A couple of firing positions would be dug in both sides of the communications trench to provide protective fire to the flanks. An angular 4–5m extension would be added to the protective trench and covered with logs and earth. This is where the section sheltered during a heavy barrage. Portions of the forward fighting trench were similarly roofed over. An entrenched latrine was added off the communications trench and other improvements made, and it is interesting to note that the Soviet manual appears to be the only one offering design details. All of these improvements depended on the time available. Besides preparing their own positions, the troops would spend a great deal of time constructing obstacles, laying mines, assisting with the construction of crew-served weapons positions and other facilities within the strongpoint, digging reserve and supplementary positions, camouflaging, general work details, standing guard, and conducting local security patrols.

There are several points to note. Most of the anti-tank guns were placed deep inside the strongpoint and oriented to protect the flanks and the gaps between adjacent strongpoints. This also protected them from being exposed to direct fire if positioned on the forward edge. Heavy machine-gun bunkers were located across the front, covering it with interlocking fire. There were one or two light machine-gun positions per section position; anti-tank rifles were scattered through the position in twos and threes, and were intended to remain mobile. The strongpoint's front was protected by an anti-tank ditch, which extended across the gaps between adjacent strongpoints. Machine gun positions were emplaced at the angles of the ditches. Enemy armour would attempt to penetrate through the gaps and this would expose them to flanking anti-tank fire from the strongpoints. Barbed wire also protected the strongpoint and its flanks. The barbed wire was open to the rear to allow counter-attacks through if the strongpoint was overrun.

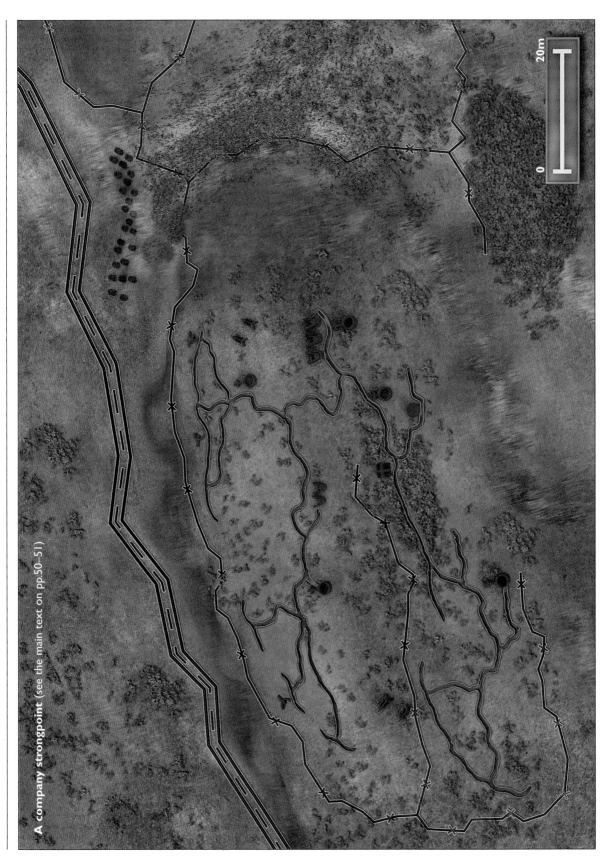

A company strongpoint (see the main text on pp.50–51)

☰☰	Anti-tank ditch	⍦	82mm mortar	■	Aid station
⤝⤟⤝	Barbed wire	♀	Platoon command post	⋏	Heavy machine gun
⇒<	45mm anti-tank gun	♀	Company command post	○ ○ ○	Anti-personnel mines
⍦	50mm mortar	●	Ammunition point	● ● ●	Anti-tank mines

The defence of cities

Soviet doctrine for the defence of large built-up areas called for extensive in-depth defences many kilometres outside the city. Stalingrad's 'outer defence belt' (O-Line) began over 100km out and was backed by a 'central defence belt' (K-Line). These focused on anti-tank defences and obstacles and were concentrated in depth along the main roads leading to the city. This wore down the enemy, allowing for more robust defences to be prepared just outside and inside the city. Large manoeuvre formations were posted between 5 and 40km to the city's flanks to prevent its envelopment. Denser belts of mines and obstacles backed by anti-tank defences supported by infantry constituted the 'inner defence belt' (S-Line). The inner defence belt actually began outside the city proper (in the suburbs), and was established on dominating terrain, taking advantage of natural obstacles.

The entire civilian population, barraged with motivational propaganda, could be mobilized, abilities permitting, to prepare defences, including those outside the city. They could also form ad hoc combat and support units. In some instances civilians were not even permitted to leave the embattled city. There are many stories of civilian families living in the basement of defended buildings and feeding and providing first aid for soldiers.

Massive enemy aerial and artillery bombardment was expected, and the attack into the city would be led by armour. Again, anti-tank defences and obstacles were established in depth throughout the city. The goal was to force the enemy to abandon the use of armour by making its use too costly, forcing him to employ

This street barricade with firing embrasures was built between two apartment blocks. Tank tracks have been incorporated into the rock and sod barricade. A shallow anti-tank ditch fronts the barricade, from which the building materials were excavated. Besides a firing position, it presents a formidable anti-tank barrier. Note that some apartment windows have been barricaded with concrete blocks, and possess embrasures. (RGAKFD)

only infantry and pioneers. Well-protected artillery positions were established deep inside the city and outside as well. The defences, as in the countryside, were built around strongpoints, aimed at channelling the attack into fire sacks. The presence of rubble and ruins aided a stubborn, prolonged defence by providing innumerable obstacles and hiding places. Burned-out buildings were not as vulnerable to incendiary bomb attacks. Strongpoints, which could be a single building of massive construction, a building complex, or an area of several blocks, were connected by trenches cut through the debris. Storm-sewer systems were utilized, and sometimes tunnels connected the basements of separate buildings. 'Switch positions' were prepared to cut off enemy penetrations; major efforts were undertaken to contain such incidents.

Anti-tank shock groups, mobile anti-tank guns, direct-fire artillery, submachine-gun groups, and large numbers of snipers were employed. The latter had a dramatic effect on enemy morale, and together with machine guns and mortars they made movement on streets virtually impossible. Efforts were made to determine where enemy assault groups were forming and to attack them with indirect fire and ground attacks from the flanks and rear; it was a three-dimensional war. Opposing forces might hold adjacent rooms and different portions of multiple-floor buildings. The Soviets attempted to wear down the enemy by constantly funnelling fresh troops and supplies into embattled cities. Every strongpoint had to be reduced at great loss. They would not be given up easily, and if lost repeated counter-attacks would be launched to re-take them. Reinforcements, replacements, and supplies would be moved up at night.

The defence of buildings

A great deal of action took place in built-up or urban areas, and not just in Stalingrad. While the defence of a three-storey apartment with basement is used as an example below, these same principles were used for preparing the defence of factories, warehouses, schools, office buildings, apartment blocks, and so on. In central parts of cities, pre-Soviet construction was generally heavy and featured thick masonry, while Stalin-era buildings were usually of massive reinforced concrete construction. The housing on the city outskirts was largely of wood.

The Red Army often avoided defending villages. They attracted artillery fire, provided little protection from it, and were prone to catching fire. Most villages were of log and wooden-frame construction, although some brick buildings were encountered. In the winter it was often necessary to shelter in villages just to survive, regardless of other risks. Fighting positions would be emplaced outside the village to take advantage of open fields of fire and avoid fire directed at the dominant buildings. Fighting positions were sometimes built underneath houses. They could be tunnelled beneath or dug into the floor and roofed over like a bunker. Inside walls were reinforced with logs and sandbags, and further supported with angled beams. Loopholes were cut through walls, usually low to the ground so fighting holes could be dug into earth floors. When the Soviets withdrew from a village they often burned it to deny its shelter and fortification-building materials to the Germans.

A battery commander's observation post was dug for each battery covering their sector of fire during static situations. It required a great deal of time and much effort to conceal from the enemy's observers, and so examples were seldom this elaborate. (US Army)

BATTERY COMMANDER'S OBSERVATION POST

The Red Army developed building defence into a fine art. Buildings would be defended from the basement up. Basements provided protection from artillery fire. The ground floor was provided additional support by buttressing with timbers and stacked masonry, sometimes wrapped with wire-mesh fencing. Existing supports were reinforced. The ground floor was covered with at least 30cm of earth or layered rubble for fire- and splinter-proofing. Slit trenches and even bunkers with overhead cover were built in basements. Slit trenches would connect firing positions within the basement (most had earth floors). Only about three-quarters of a basement was below ground. The above-ground portion had narrow casemate windows, or loopholes could be cut for anti-tank weapons and machine guns. Command posts, aid stations, and ammunition and supplies storage were located in the basements. If a second exit from the basement did not exist, one would be prepared.

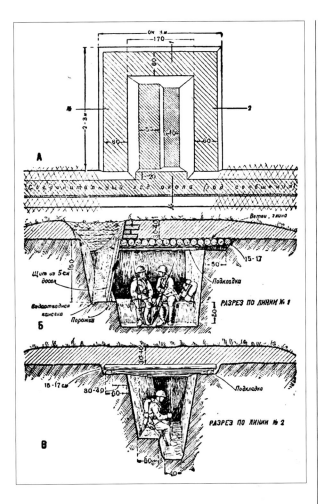

This type of dugout could shelter three or four men. It was of the cut-and-fill type being dug down from ground level, having the roof installed, and then being backfilled. It could be dug completely from ground level, or once the roof was installed and covered the soldier 'tunnelled' beneath the roof. (Author's collection)

Loopholes were cut though walls, including dummy ones, which were painted to draw fire. If windows were used for firing from, the shooter would be inside the building to prevent him from being seen and to conceal muzzle flash and the sound of the report. Ground-floor windows were blocked with planks or strung with barbed wire or wire mesh to keep out attackers and grenades. Bed frames with wire mesh were used for the same purpose. Fragmentation and anti-tank hand grenades were thrown from upper-storey windows. All windows had the glass removed to prevent injuries from flying glass. Exterior doors were barricaded and unused stairwells blocked by throwing furniture and wreckage down them. They were sometimes booby-trapped with trip-wire grenades. It was common practice to enter and exit a building through windows or mouse-holes, as snipers often watched over the doors. Firing positions were built of sandbags and rubble low on the floor, not just behind the exterior walls, but also to protect the position's sides and overhead. Tables were used for the latter, with sandbags stacked on top and on the floor as well. Bed mattresses were used as splinter shields. Buckets of sand were placed at intervals to extinguish fires, and curtains and other flammable materials were removed. Ammunition, rations, water, and medical supplies were stockpiled. Mouse-holes were knocked or blasted through walls and floors to connect rooms (blocks of buildings often had common side walls).

Observers, snipers, and radio positions were emplaced in the upper floors and attics. Mortars were set up on flat-roofed buildings or holes were knocked through roofs. Sandbagged platforms were prepared for mortars and if necessary support beams positioned on the floor below. Defended buildings were connected by trenches, covered with planks and rubble. Adjacent buildings might be burned, levelled, or the facing walls blown off to expose the interior to the defenders' fire. Alleyways were barricaded and booby-trapped.

One example of the resolute defence of a building is Pavlov's House in northern Stalingrad. Dom Pavlova was a block-long, heavily constructed, four-storey, masonry apartment house overlooking 9th of January Square. On September 23, 1941 a Soviet platoon seized this building 250m from the River Volga. Senior Sergeant Yakov Pavlov and three men survived to defend the building against repeated German counter-attacks. After several desperate days,

A defended building

The Red Army developed building defence techniques into an art. This three-storey apartment building features many of the typical defensive methods. In the basement (1) a 45mm anti-tank gun has been mounted on a timber platform to fire through a casemate window. A trench across the basement floor (2) connects to a bunker occupied by the gun crew during heavy shelling. A covered trench (3) links the building to another. A Maxim machine gun is mounted in a window on a sandbag platform (4). The floor is covered with soil for fire- and splinter-proofing. Various means are used to block windows – including barbed-wire screens, an upturned bed frame (5), and sandbags (6). A knife-rest wire obstacle blocks the stairwell door (7), and furniture has been dumped into the stairwell. On the second floor rifle loopholes have been knocked through walls, and grenadiers prepare to lob grenades through the windows (8). Mouse-holes (9) have been cut through floors and interior walls to allow access to adjacent rooms. On the third floor snipers and observers are posted (10). In the attic (11) an 82mm mortar has been set up, and an opening has been cut through the roof. The floor is reinforced by a sandbag platform, and timbers on the floor below (12) provide additional support.

reinforcements arrived with anti-tank rifles, machine guns, ammunition, and supplies. This large structure was still only defended by 25 men. They surrounded the building with mines and barbed wire and undertook most of the defensive measures previously described. Trenches were dug to other Soviet positions and the strongpoint was supplied by boats crossing the river. The Germans subjected the crumbling building to continuous fire and day and night attacks, suffering great losses in the process. One end of the building completely collapsed. Pavlov's House was key to preventing the Germans from reaching the river in this sector. The few surviving defenders were relieved on November 25 after 63 days.

Another desperate battle for a building took place at the massive concrete grain elevator near the river in southern Stalingrad. Its 50 defenders had two Maxim machine guns and two anti-tank rifles. They held the elevator from September 14 to 20 fighting off 10–14 counter-attacks a day. The grain caught fire and burned for days, creating billowing grey smoke; there was no water to extinguish this. The smoke was so dense that part of the structure had to be abandoned. Finally – having run out of water, grenades, and machine-gun and anti-tank ammunition – they were overwhelmed, but a handful of survivors broke out. The fighting had been so vicious at the grain elevator that the German Field Marshal Paulus used it as the centrepiece symbol on the Stalingrad Badge he ordered designed; it was never produced.

Forest and swamp defences

The Germans tended to avoid combat in forests if possible, and for good reason. The Soviets proved able to conduct an effective defence in such locations, and it was here that they often executed their most resolute efforts. The Germans preferred to by-pass smaller forested areas, seeking instead to conduct decisive battles in open terrain where they held a distinct advantage. By-passed forests would be mopped up later as the main Soviet forces were pushed back. Such mop-ups were time consuming and comparatively costly. It was common to simply leave by-passed holdouts to wither on the vine. In other instances the Germans intentionally drove defeated Soviet troops into swamps, where it was thought they would starve and eventually surrender. The Germans soon found that today's by-passed pocket became tomorrow's partisan band.

The Red Army soldiers had a reputation for selecting mutually supporting positions, good camouflage, the use of decoy positions, integrating natural obstacles, and digging in. Most armies defended the forward edge of the tree-line, or just inside it, to provide them with wide fields of observation and fire.

A 152mm M-1910/30 howitzer, mainly assigned to second-line formations, is emplaced in a typical artillery position. The camouflage net does little to conceal the exposed parapet and equipment around the position, but does deny observers from determining the type of weapon. (RGAKFD)

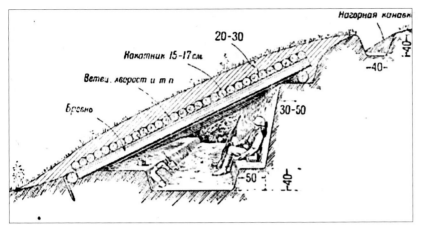

Нагорная канова

20-30

Накатник 15-17 см

Ветви, хворост и т п

Бревно

-40-

30-50

-50-

This type of personnel shelter was built on reverse slopes. It required a good deal of digging and a large number of logs. Note the drainage deflection trench dug upslope. These were dug above hillside fighting trenches as well. (Author's collection)

In contrast, the Soviets dug their main defensive positions deep inside the forest. There were a number of valid reasons for doing this:

• It did not provide the enemy with a landmark or obvious line on which the defences were built.
• It hid the defensive positions from enemy aerial observation and air attack.
• It denied enemy armour the ability to manoeuvre once inside the forest.
• It forced enemy infantry to fight dismounted, and to use only short-range direct fire and close assault methods.
• It was difficult for the enemy to coordinate and adjust indirect fire owing to few landmarks and limited visibility.
• Being hidden inside the forest, direct-fire artillery and tank fire could not be brought to bear on their positions.
• There were few clearings in which the enemy could set up and fire mortars and artillery.
• It was difficult for advancing enemy troops to remain oriented and maintain contact with adjacent units.
• Logistics and communications for the attacker were complicated.
• Fortification and obstacle construction materials were plentiful.

The defending Soviets would position outposts (some containing anti-tank rifles and guns) on the tree-line and even forward of it to warn of the enemy's approach, to direct artillery fire, and to hinder enemy patrols. Further outposts were placed inside the forest, and ambushes and snipers harassed the advancing enemy. It was here in particular that such outposts might be placed in lines diagonal to the MLR to further disorient the enemy. Roads and tracks were scarce and seldom marked on what maps were available. Aerial photography was of little help as the canopy hid trails and landmarks.

The Germans were at a disadvantage in the forests and swamps. They were not trained for forest fighting and relied on supporting weapons such as heavy machine guns, mortars, infantry guns, anti-tank guns, artillery, and dive-bombers. In the forests, they now had to rely on platoon weapons only. Heavy machine guns were used in the light role and positioned forward with the assault troops. To make matters worse, the deeply dug-in log and earth fortifications required heavy weapons to reduce them; only light weapons were available though. The Soviets did not clear obvious fields of fire within forests, but sparingly cleared only low underbrush, lower twigs, and branches of vegetation. As a result, the Germans would frequently walk unknowingly into fire zones. The latter were laid out so that the fire would come from different directions to confuse the attackers even more. Some positions were situated to take the advancing enemy under fire from the rear and flanks. Such short-range engagements were morale shattering, owing to the confusion and their apparent impotence as the habitual supporting weapons were not available. The Germans simply did not like close-range engagements and the high cost in casualties. Over time they developed forest fighting tactics and techniques, and conducted appropriate training, but it was still a tough environment.

The many lakes, swamps, and bogs found in forests allowed the Soviets to integrate these into their obstacle plan. In some areas these were so dense that they needed only screening forces to protect them. Because German penetrations were usually small and often occurred in multiple areas, the Soviets retained numerous small reserves. An effective and easy to create forest obstacle was the abatis. This could be used to block roads and trails, and bands of trees across the front could be felled with the interlocking limbs toward the enemy. Some trees would be left standing to make the obstacle less conspicuous to aerial observers. Barbed wire and booby traps might be installed among the limbs.

Many of the forests and water courses turned into swamps in the spring and autumn. High water tables meant positions had to be built above ground. Positions could be built atop small islands, which had to be built up using logs, bundles of limbs or reeds, and imported soil and blocks of peat. Timber fighting positions were built on log rafts and could be moved to new locations. Soil might be man-packed from nearby dry ground to build high, revetted, double-walled parapets that formed trenches. Mud was scooped out of shallow waters, mixed with pine needles, and dried for use in parapets. Mines could not generally be used in these areas.

Winter defences

With heavy snowfall and freezing conditions, existing fortifications had to be modified, special positions constructed, and obstacles rebuilt. Embrasures had to be raised above snow level as it got deeper. This required trenches and fighting position floors to be filled in with earth; the sides built up with logs, earth, and packed snow; and the roofs raised. Uncovered trenches were often covered with logs. The angle of incline had to be kept low (25 per cent) to prevent snow drifting and overloading trench covers with weight, and creating drifts that signalled the location of positions. Fighting positions that could not be modified were adapted as quarters and supply shelters. Embrasures were sealed with sandbags or straw mats and doors or curtains fitted. Heating means were installed if possible. In extremely deep snow, trenches and positions could be dug into the snow and the outside packed in layers. Roughly 1.3–1.8m of packed snow backed by brushwood latticework provided protection from small-arms fire. Bunkers and other positions with overhead cover were built in the normal manner, but layers of insulating materials were added between

A winter-quarters shelter made of snow blocks and covered with packed snow which has been blown smooth by the wind. Underneath there is probably a layer of evergreen needles, straw, or other material for insulation. (Nik Cornish at Stavka)

layers of logs, earth, and packed snow. This included sawdust, wood-shavings, finely chopped fir twigs, pine needles, and peat moss.

Snow was a plentiful commodity during the Russian winter, though the duration and depth of snowfall varied depending on the locality. In the north it began in December and accumulated 100cm or more, and remained into June. In the south it began in January and remained until April with only 10–40cm falling. With temperatures remaining between -30 and -45°C through the winter, ice blocks and packed snow were very useful for constructing fortifications and shelters. Often these were the only materials available. Ice and packed snow was bulletproof (though armour-piercing rounds achieved better penetration), easily camouflaged, and easy to work with. The only tools necessary were standard shovels, hatchets, axes, and crowbars. Broader snow shovels and ice saws were sometimes available. Different types of snow provided varying degrees of protection from small-arms fire (see Table 4).

The Soviets developed a number of mixtures of ice concrete made of frozen water and sand or crushed rock. It was extremely hard, but it was difficult to prepare and shape, and so was not widely used. Frozen mixtures of clay and sand were also used. Ice and ice concrete were suitable for building rear-area structures; however, because they were so brittle they created a splinter hazard when struck by bullets.

In deep snow, trenches were prepared by columns of men tramping the snow down deeper and deeper as the column progressed from one fighting position and bunker to the next. A frozen crust would form on the trench sides overnight. Barbed-wire obstacles could still be effective even if covered by drifting snow as the extent and layout of the wire was hidden. The abatis was also an effective obstacle in winter snows.

This museum exhibit displays the interior of a *zemlyanki* winter-quarters shelter. Those behind the lines were usually provided with small windows for ventilation. The shelves are made from ammunition crates. (Nik Cornish at Stavka)

Table 4: Minimum thickness for protection from small-arms fire

Material	Minimum thickness in cm/in.
Loose snow	305cm/120in.
Packed snow	200cm/80in.
Frozen crust snow	100–150cm/40–60in.
Ice	70cm/28in.
Frozen soil	50cm/20in.
Ice concrete	30cm/12in.

An assessment of Soviet field fortifications

By the time of the pivotal battle of Kursk in July 1943, the Red Army had reached its zenith in the development of defensive works and tactics. From that point on the Soviets moved to the offensive, adopting many of the principles of German tactics. The need for massive strongpoints and elaborate, in-depth obstacle systems was reduced, but there were still many sectors in which units assumed the defence, even if for a brief time.

Generally, the design of Soviet field fortifications displayed few innovations and little imagination. They were very simple and provided only the most basic amenities, particularly with regard to crew-served weapons. For example, a simple design for the mortar pit was provided for all variants – only the dimensions changed. There were very few designs for specialized bunkers and shelters. Although on paper they lacked a certain robustness, in practice they tended to be constructed more heavily. As it was, troops took great liberty in their construction and design, incorporating lessons learned.

A notable feature of Soviet fortifications was their extent, the way they supported other positions, and the integration of obstacles. As experience was gained, their design improved and troops became more resourceful. Winter positions were well designed and numerous innovations were seen. It was also realized by higher commands that heating and other improvements had to be provided for winter positions in order for the defenders to survive, for frostbite and other cold injuries to be reduced, and to continue the defence effectively.

Avenues of approach and obstacles (including minefields) needed to be kept under constant observation to prevent surprise attacks. Camouflage and concealment, including deception measures, from both ground and air observation were essential. The overall layout and layering of defences in depth was essential to a successful defence, as was the maximum use of available local materials. The Soviets excelled in all these areas.

Field fortifications by their very nature are temporary. In the years since World War II, farming, creeping urbanization, and land clearing have covered over many of the remaining fortifications in the former Soviet Union. Yet in many remote areas, or even just outside rural villages, remnants of fortifications and obstacles can still be found, both crudely built trenches and bunkers and reinforced concrete pillboxes. Their German counterparts are to be found with them, some built one on top of the other. Today, a number of amateur fortification archaeological groups are seeking to locate and excavate these sites. These sometimes yield deteriorating artefacts, which are mostly cleaned and donated to local museums for preservation.

Battlefield tours are available today in such areas as St. Petersburg (formerly Leningrad), Moscow, Kursk, Volgograd (formerly Stalingrad), and other sites, and some old fortifications and obstacles can be seen. One example is Pavlov's House in Volgograd. The collapsed end was rebuilt from recovered bricks, but is still in a destroyed, roofless condition and stands as a memorial.

Further reading and research

Only limited post-war study has been undertaken of Soviet field fortifications. Most of the information available on Soviet field fortifications was obtained from German wartime intelligence, much of which was turned over to the US Army immediately after the war. Even in 1945 there was sufficient concern for the United States to increase intelligence collection on the USSR.

Biryukov, G. and Melnikov, G. *Anti-tank Warfare*. Moscow: Progress Publishers, 1972.

Kaufmann, J. E. and Kaufmann, H. W. *Fortress Europe: European Fortifications of World War II*. Cambridge, MA: De Capo Press, 2002.

Sharp, Charles S. *Soviet Infantry Tactics in World War II: Red Army Infantry Tactics from Squad to Rifle Company from the Combat Regulations*. West Chester, OH: Nafziger Collection, 1998.

Strategy and Tactics Staff *War in the East: The Russo-German Conflict, 1941–45*. New York: Simulations Publications, 1977.

Tsouras, Peter G. (editor) *Fighting in Hell: The German Ordeal on the Eastern Front*. London: Greenhill Books, 1995. (This is a compilation of reprinted US Army studies written by former German officers.)

US Army *Handbook on USSR Military Forces, TM 30-430*, November 1946.

Zaloga, Steven J. and Ness, Leland S. *Red Army Handbook, 1939–1945*. Gloucestershire: Sutton Publishing, 1998.

Glossary and abbreviations

AFV Armoured fighting vehicle (i.e. a tank, assault gun, halftrack, armoured car, or reconnaissance vehicle).

Fire sack Also known as a 'fire trap' or 'anti-tank area', these were ambush sites on routes that armour might follow if it broke through and continued into a rear area.

FOG A fixed flamethrower.

frontoviki Frontline soldiers.

HE High explosive.

HMG Heavy machine gun.

Isba A log cabin.

LMG Light machine gun.

MLR Main line of resistance.

Protivotankovyy Rezerv Anti-tank reserve.

Ukreplennye Raiony A fortified region.

zemlyanki Shelters used for winter quarters by Soviet troops, based on the traditional *zemlyanki* built by serfs – pit houses dug into the ground.

Index

AFV positions 19, 30, **45, 51**
anti-tank battalions 23–4
anti-tank defences 7–11, 18–19
   see also anti-tank gun positions;
      anti-tank guns; ditches: anti-tank;
      rifle positions: anti-tank
anti-tank gun positions
   cities **56–7**
   countryside 19, 30, 37–9, **38, 40**
anti-tank guns 9, 21, **40**, 51
artillery
   camouflage **47**
   commanders' observation posts **41, 54**
   German 29
   organization 24
   quality and transport 21
   ranges 24
   self-propelled 19
   uses 8–9, 19–20
   see also individual types by name

barbed wire 27
building defences 54–8, **56–7**
bunkers
   for machine guns 21, **23, 35**
   mini-bunkers 24
   as troop shelters **42, 44–5, 44, 55**

camouflage 12, 20, 27, 40, 46–9, **47, 49**
   nets **8, 19**, 29, 31, 46, 47
carbines **51**
city defences 53–8, **53, 56–7**
climate 5, 61
communications 50
concrete 25, 61
construction
   ditches 4
   labour 4, 12–13
   materials 25–7
   principles 28–30
   riflemen's positions **6–7**
   strongpoints 50–1

defensive doctrine 4, 6–11
   centralized and decentralized defence 9–11
   lack of mobility 11
   timing of firing 13
ditches: anti-tank 4, 10, 16–17
dugouts **42, 44–5, 44, 55**
dummy fortifications 9, 12, 49

earth sod blocks 26–7
entrances 29

field guns **47**
fire sacks 8
firing embrasures 29, **29–30, 43**
flamethrowers 20
forest defences 58–60
frontages and depths 14–15

German Army: tactics against fortifications
   20, 59–60
grenades **30**

hedgehogs **33**
howitzers **58**

ice concrete 61

machine-gun battalions 23
machine-gun positions 33–6
   anti-aircraft 34
   in anti-tank trenches **10**, 34
   bunkers 21, **23, 35**
   in cities **56–7**
   cut-and-fill **20**
   for heavy machine guns **16–17, 19**
   for light machine guns **15, 18**
   positioning **13**
   in section trenches **42–3**
   in strongpoints 51
   for submachine guns **33**
machine guns
   anti-aircraft 34
   light machine guns **15, 18**
   Maxims 23, 34, **35**
   submachine guns **11, 30, 33**
   types 23
main lines of resistance see MLRs
mines 20
mini-bunkers **24**
MLRs (main lines of resistance) 14–15
Molotov Line 5
mortar positions
   cities **56–7**
   countryside 36–7, **37, 39**
mortars 22–3, **37**

observation posts **41, 47, 54**
obstacles
   types 22
   see also individual types by name
outpost lines 14
outposts, combat 7–8

positioning 14–20, 28, 48, 50
Pripet Marshes 5

rail system 5
Red Army
   organization 21–4

preparedness for *Barbarossa* 12
   toughness 20
   transport 21–2
revetments 30
rifle battalions 22–3, 33
rifle brigades 24
rifle companies 23
rifle divisions 21–4
rifle platoons 23, 33
rifle positions: anti-tank **9–12, 15**, 32
rifle regiments 22
riflemen's positions **6–8**, 31–2, **42**, 51
rifles **9, 11–12**, 18–19, 23, 32
rivers 5
roads 5
rock 27
roofs 28–9, **35**, 45

sandbags 26
security lines 14
shelters **42, 44–6, 44, 55, 59–61**
snow: protective qualities 61
Stalin Line 5
Stalingrad: defences 53, 55–8, **56–7**
stone 27
strongpoints 8–9, 15–16, 28,
   50–1, **52**
swamp defences 58–60

tanks **45, 49, 51**
terrain 5
timber 25
Timoshenko, Marshal Semyon 6
tools **27–8**
trenches 5, 39–44
   and anti-tank gun positions 37
   in cities **56–7**
   communications **32**
   construction 28, 29
   crawl **27**
   cross-sections 31
   fighting 26
   as machine-gun positions 34–6
   and mortar positions 37, **39**
   revetments 30
   section 31, **42–3**
   and strongpoints 51
   types and dimensions **25**, 40–1
Tukhachevsky, Marshal Mikhail 6

village defences 54

weapons
   organization 21–4
   positioning 18
   types used against tanks 8–9
   see also individual types by name
winter defences 60–1, **60–1**, 62